AMERICAN CATHOLICS SINCE THE COUNCIL

An Unauthorized Report

Andrew M. Greeley

THE THOMAS MORE PRESS
Chicago, Illinois

ISBN 0-88347-191-4

CONTENTS

CHAPTER ONE

Introduction

This book is about the present condition of American Catholics. It is not a book of opinion but a book of facts, facts assembled on the twentieth anniversary of the end of the Second Vatican Council and in preparation for the synod of bishops in Rome in the Autumn of 1985 to review the work of the Vatican Council and its impact on Catholics throughout the world.

The data on which this unauthorized and unsolicited report are based have been collected over the last twenty years by my colleagues and myself at the National Opinion Research Center. However, this book is not intended to be a social science monograph with statistical tables, sociological terminology, and complex mathematical models. Those who wish more technical information or more precise validation of the present report can find such materials in a number of publications -- The Education of Catholic Americans, Catholic Schools in a Declining Church , Crisis in the Church, The Young Catholic Family, The American Catholic: A Social Portrait, The Young Catholic, The Religious Imagination, Angry Catholic Women, and Religion: Social Indicators. Only the last volume is not yet published. Moreover all of the analysis is based on data in the public domain and much of it on materials in NORC's annual General Social Survey which are on line in most university computer centers.

The reader who will not want to be bothered with socio-logical technicalities will have to assume that I am both professionally honest and technically competent, and that the factual portrait I present is accurate and is based on the best possible social science data. All assertions in this book are based on national probability samples designed by and interviews conducted by one of the country's oldest, most able social science research centers. I intend to speculate about the meaning of some of the data that I will present, but I will distinguish sharply in the text so that the reader will know when I am reporting and when I am in-terpreting. Only in the conclusion will I go beyond the facts and speculations closely connected to facts to offer my own general interpretation of what the facts mean.

No one is without personal biases or opinions when the subject is Catholicism. Objectivity does not mean indiffer-ence or neutrality, it merely means an awareness of one's own propensities and proclivities and determination not to let them interfere with the accurate reporting of the socio-logical evidence. For my own integrity in these matters I

will cite two cases (in line with St. Paul's observation
that I ought not boast but if boast I must):

1. In the early 1970s I realized that the finding in
our study on the Catholic priesthood that more than four-
fifths of American Catholic priests rejected the Church's
birth control teaching would make me permanently unacceptable to the Catholic hierarchy, especially since they funded
the study which produced the finding. Nonetheless, I
reported the finding, not because I necessarily agreed with
the attitudes of my fellow priests on the subject but
because I felt I had a professional obligation to report the
facts.

Fifteen years later when I set out to examine General
Social Survey data collected by the National Opinion
Research Center and prove that the bishop's pastoral on nuclear weapons had no effect at all on American Catholics, I
discovered to my astonishment (as I shall report in this
book) that just the opposite was the case and that the bishop's pastoral letter on nuclear weapons was one of the most
effective educational interventions that social science has
ever discovered. After a decade and a half of being rejected by the leadership of my church for having told the truth
about birth control, I am certainly disinclined to give them
credit for anything. I stared blankly at my computer screen

with the astonishing numbers and realized that it was the same temptation that I had experienced on the subject of priests and birth control fifteen years before.

Thus, as best I can I report the facts as they are, not as I would like them to be. More than that, no one can do.

Some preliminary comments are in order, however, to set down the boundaries of the present work.

1. I have sharply distinguished in my work on this book between fact and value, between the way things are and the way they ought to be. This is a distinction which most bishops, many priests, and not a few Catholic laity, do not seem to be able to accept or even comprehend. If I report, for example, that the majority of American Catholics can live easily with a married clergy, this does not mean that I personally advocate a married clergy (in this particular case, I would be part of the minority opposed to the abandonment of clerical celibacy). Nor does it follow because my data indicate that four-fifths of American Catholics no longer think that premarital sex is always wrong that I think the church should change its teaching on premarital sex to, as has often been suggested, "keep the laity happy."

When my colleagues and I prepare a report about American Catholicism we ALWAYS insert a qualification that we do not believe that ethical values can be obtained by counting noses. Surveys are a useful technique for finding out what people are thinking and doing, but they are not a technique for arriving at morally desirable norms for behavior. Nonetheless, it always seems that someone promptly issues a statement critical of our report in which it is reasserted that the Catholic Church does not arrive at moral decisions by taking surveys -- implying that my colleagues and I have suggested that it should.

Moral principles are not determined by votes, by surveys, by popularity contests. Anyone who suggests that I believe that they are is deliberately distorting my stated and explicit conviction. Understandably perhaps, bishops are tempted by the Old Testament practice of killing the herald that brings the bad news. He who reports to you the existence of problems is the ideal one to scapegoat as the cause of the problem. Thus, a certain prominent archbishop has blamed me for the laity's change of mind on birth control after the Humanae Vitae encyclical, not at all impeded in assigning such blame by the fact that my report on the change in Catholic birth control attitudes appeared EIGHT YEARS AFTER THE ENCYCLICAL. If you feel frustrated and powerless, however, you must blame someone and you might just as well blame the social scientist. He makes an excellent scapegoat.

Pope John Paul in his exhortation _Familiaris_
Consortio observes that the married laity, through the
charism of the sacrament of matrimony, have a unique and indispensable contribution to make to the church's self-
understanding of marital morality. He also says in the same
context that while social surveys are useful and necessary
and good, they are not the only way of discovering what the
sense of the faithful is on these matters.

Some of my friends and some of my enemies have suggested that the Pope wrote these paragraphs with me in mind, implicitly condemning me and my work. It is possible that the
Pope did indeed have me in mind when he drafted those paragraphs (I would be flattered if he did).

It is also possible that he intended the words to be a
condemnation of my work (I would be disappointed if he did),
but in fact, the pope only repeated my own opinion, and
indeed, a position which I have taken in public repeatedly.
The lay people have a unique and indispensable contribution
to make to the church's self-understanding. This "sense of
the faithful" is not obtained merely by social research,
though social research may make a useful and partial
contribution to know what is the "sense of the faithful."

In the first thousand years and more of Catholic history, it would have been taken for granted that the laity

would be consulted on all matters of importance to the Church. In the early days, even in Rome, an elected bishop (selected by the parish priests) would be brought out on the balcony to be appraised by the people of the city. If they cheered, he was confirmed. If they booed, the parish priests (even the cardinals, if it was Rome) scurried back into the cathedral to have another vote. One does not advocate a return to such practices when one insists that it is sound traditional Catholic doctrine that the Holy Spirit is at work among the laity as well as among the clergy and the hierarchy and that, as the document on the church at the Second Vatican Council stated forcefully, one of the most important roles of the bishop is to "discern" the spirit at work among the laity. Social research then is useful not as a tool for moral decision making, nor as a means for determining what will make the laity happy so that the church may keep its laity happy.

Social research, rather, is an instrument useful and perhaps in this day even necessary for church leaders to use in the discernment of the spirit, for a careful and sensitive attempt to see what the Holy Spirit may be trying to say to church leaders through the faith. If one cannot distinguish between making moral decisions by majority vote on the one hand and listening to discern the spirit at work

among the laity on the other, one simply is not very
sensitive either religiously or sociologically.

I do not believe, for example, that the church should
have changed its birth control teaching merely because the
lay people wanted it changed or merely to keep the lay people happy. But I do believe that the church leadership has
failed to listen carefully enough to what the married laity
have said about the importance of sex in their marriage and
about the relationship between sex and procreation. I quite
agree with John Paul II that the married lay people have, in
virtue of the charism of the sacrament of matrimony, a
unique and indispensable contribution to make to the
church's self-understanding. My problem is I don't think
that they have been given a chance in this last quarter century to make such a contribution. I would not contend that
survey research is the only way for the laity's insights to
be shared with the clergy and the hierarchy on the meaning
of sex in marriage, but I do believe that social surveys are
one way that the voice of the laity might be heard, a good
and useful and perhaps necessary way, unfortunately also
often a shocking and painful instrument of upward
communication.

This report is mostly about the Catholic laity, not
about the clergy or the religious. Many more studies have

been made of the lay response to the Vatican Council than of
the clerical response. Generally speaking the quality of the
research evidence on the laity is much better than that from
studies of the clergy. Moreover, the council has affected
the laity in a very different way than it has affected the
clergy and religious. It seems to me to be important on the
twentieth anniversary of the end of the council and in preparation for the extraordinary synod of bishops to concentrate in this book on the laity only because the picture for
the laity is less complex and more readily documented.

It must be remembered however, that the ordinary lay
person does not read theology books or Catholic journals;
indeed, the typical American Catholic lay person has probably never read a document from the Second Vatican Council.
The laity's impression of the changes in the church are collected from newspapers, news magazines, television programs,
and radio news casts. Moreover, many if not most of the issues about which the fathers of the council agonized -- col-
legiality, the inspiration of scripture, religious freedom,
liturgy -- are of small practical impact on the lives of the
ordinary lay person. For the laity, the most striking phenomena are Mass in English, meat on Friday, greater ease for
divorced Catholics to remarry, better relationships with
Protestants and Jews, a more relaxed atmosphere in the

relationship between priests and lay people, priests and
nuns leaving the active ministry, an environment of flow, if
not instability, in the church and in their parish. The
impact of the Vatican Council, such as it may have been, on
Catholic laity is almost entirely mediated through the mass
media, through the occasional and not always coherent
remarks of their religious leaders, and through the
atmosphere and environment of the local church, particularly
parish and diocese. It might be desirable perhaps for the
lay reaction to the council to have been more intricate,
complex, and theologically sophisticated, but in fact to the
average Catholic layman, the principal impression of the
Second Vatican Council is probably that a lot of things that
he or she thought were unchangeable, have been, for better
or for worse, changed.

That a change has occurred since the end of the Vatican
Council does not mean that the council has caused the
change. For example, the Catholic divorce rate has increased notably in the last twenty years. It is unlikely
that this increase is the result either of the changes in-
troduced by the Vatican Council or by the modernization of
the church's annulment procedures. The divorce rates of all
Americans have increased notably in the last twenty years,
Protestant and Jewish divorce rates no more precipitously

than Catholic divorce rates. The most likely explanation
for this change is that women now have both control of their
own fertility because of the birth control pill and financial independence because of their positions in the work
force. It is easier for a woman to escape from a difficult
and unhappy marriage than it was twenty-five years ago. The
increase in divorce rate merely means an increase in the
proportion of women who are leaving marriages that they find
unsatisfactory, not necessarily an increase in the number of
unsatisfactory marriages. The divorce rate tells nothing
about the quality of marriages which do not end in divorce
-- thus the use of the divorce rate as an indicator of the
"decline of the family" is a logical fallacy.

It is possible that the changes since the Second
Vatican Council have enabled Catholics to seek divorces with
an easier conscience than would have been possible in the
era before the council. However, if there is such change in
conscience it has not made the Catholic divorce rate increase more precipitously than the general divorce rate in
American society has increased.

Moreover, the proportion of Catholics attending and
graduating from college has increased tremendously in the
last quarter century, from twenty-five percent of American
collegians being Catholic in the early 1960s, to almost for-

ty-five percent in the middle 1980s. In 1960 Catholics
graduated from college at about the rate of the national
population. In 1985 it appears Catholics will graduate at a
rate close to twice their proportion in the national
population. This is obviously a change after the Second
Vatican Council, but it is equally obviously not a change
caused by the Vatican Council.

Catholics have never been obligated to believe in the
inspiration of the scripture in the same fundamentalist
sense as many Protestants. The decline in belief of literal
interpretation, measured by surveys in the last twenty
years, has been concentrated almost entirely in the Catholic
segment of the population. Is this decline caused by the
better education of American Catholics? Or is it caused by
understanding among American Catholics of the document on
revelation approved by the father's of the Second Vatican
Council? Or is it perhaps a combination of both? Have
Catholics who attended Catholic universities learned a little bit more about the Catholic doctrine on the inspiration
of the scripture since the conciliar document and therefore
become more sophisticated in their understanding of what
revelation means? The empirical evidence is ambiguous.
Changes in attitudes on the inspiration of the scripture
have taken place at all age levels in the Catholic popula-

tion but especially among younger Catholics. Forced to
speculate about the interpretation of the data, one might be
inclined to say that both the council and the social change
of more education have made their contribution to an increase in sophistication about divine revelation in the
scriptures and that probably the increased education
attainment had something more to do with the change than the
documents of the Vatican Council.

Thus any discussion of the impact of the Second
Vatican Council on American Catholics must take into account
the possibility that changes (such as attitudes towards the
literal inspiration of the scripture for example) are not
the result of the council but the result of other changes
occurring in American society.

There are four different "models" or "analytic par-
adigms" that are normally used in discussion of religious
behavior:

1. The long-term decline or "secularization" model.
In its most simple form this model views religious behavior
as declining in modern society under the impact of scientif-
ic progress, education, modernization, urbanization, and in-
dustrialization. Men and women today are less religious
than they used to be, it is frequently said, particularly in
the mass media. Or, alternatively in the Catholic perspec-

tive, our parents and grandparents were good Catholics and we are not and our children are worse than we are. The decline in Catholic practice since the Second Vatican Council, should there be any such, is attributed to the council's breaking down the barriers between Catholics and the powerful dynamisms in contemporary culture which produce secularization.

2. The cyclical model. Religion, like everything else, goes through "phases" or "cycles." There are periods of religious revival and religious decline, of "secularization" and "resacralization." The years during and immediately after the Second World War were times of a religious revival; the sixties and the early seventies were a time of religious decline; the late seventies and the early eighties are another time of religious revival.

3. The continuity model. Religion, it is argued in this perspective, is intrinsic to the human condition. As long as men and women worry about what life means, there will be religion. While there may be some rise and fall of religious behavior, the striking phenomenon about religion is how stable it is over time. "Secularization" is at most an epiphenomenon.

4. The "single jolt" model. In this perspective sometimes there are changes that are simply changes, neither cy-

clic nor long-term decline. Something happens that has a
strong effect on religious behavior, this effect is absorbed
and religious behavior continues either at a higher or lower
level than before because of the impact of this single
event.

In most discussion of contemporary American religion,
the first two models are by far the more popular because
they have more media appeal and because they give the impression that the one who is discussing them has a certain
amount of sophisticated wisdom. Theories about long-term
cycles or long term decline both influenced by overarching
-- if vague and nameless -- social forces , sound reasonable
and plausible, particularly in a society in which such ideas
as "future shock" are common and popular. We all know that
things are changing, don't we? Is it not therefore useful
and wise and good to have explanations which take into account the changes in religion and locate these religious
changes in the context of the broader, overarching and enormously powerful forces that are daily or weekly or monthly
or at least yearly reshaping our lives?

On the other hand, there is a certain absence of appeal
in both the continuity and single experience models.
Discontinuity is news, continuity is not. If you want to
have a quick explanation of the "big picture" you will find

trends and cycles more appealing than changes which simply happen more or less as historical accidents and have a limited impact which is neither cyclic nor long term. Such events offend our sense of the neatness in the order and the rhythms that are or at least ought to be in the world.

The social scientist who deals with numbers, is skeptical about cycles and long term trends until he finds data to confirm that such phenomena are in fact occurring. Thus, he'll believe in the religious revival after the Second World War and the religious decline in the sixties and seventies when he finds evidence of it. In the absence of such evidence, he will be politely agnostic.

In this report there are traces of all four phenomena. There are some long-term trends among American Catholics (most notably in their attitudes on certain sexual matters); there are a few cycles (a slight hint that church attendance which went down drastically, may be inching up again); there was a fascinating one-shot jolt which dramatically affected church attendance between 1969 and 1975. Mostly, however, this book will report stability and continuity. There have been important changes in the religious and religiously related social attitudes and behaviors of American Catholics over the last twenty years, but what is surprising, considering the enormous transformation the

Second Vatican Council accomplished, is how much stability and continuity there continues to be in the American Catholic population. For example, as will be noted later, in work that Michael Hout and I have been doing with complex mathematical models to measure defections from the Catholic Church in the last twenty years we find no trace that either the defection rate or the religious intermarriage rate changed since the late 1960s. Fifteen percent of those who were born Catholic had in 1970 defected from the Catholic Church. In 1984 the defection rate was exactly the same.

The figures give a hint of a theme that will run through the book and which will be returned to for substantial discussion in the final chapter: the loyalty of American Catholics to their religious tradition, even in this time of enormous crisis, is extremely powerful, perhaps the most important single factor one must comprehend if one is to understand the American Catholic phenomenon. In a single sentence summary: Neither the Democratic party nor the Catholic Church have been able to drive American Catholics out of either institution.

Finally, I will appeal frequently in this book to my own theoretical approach to the sociology of religion which focuses on the religious imagination. It is not my inten-

tion in this report to persuade the reader that my theory is
"right"; I shall be content with the proposition that the
theory is useful: it generates testable hypotheses about
religious phenomena and provides a framework for ordering
empirical findings. "Theory" in social science is a tentative and provisional non-exclusive paradigm for ordering and
explaining data. My "theory" of religion sees religion taking its origins and its raw power from experiences which renew hope; these experiences are encoded in human memories
through residual images called symbols; these symbols are
shared with others in stories; and these stories are told
to narrative communities in which the members have common
story telling symbols. Specifically, for the purposes of
this volume, the theory can be summarized by saying that if
one knows how a respondent pictures God, one can make a number of extremely useful predictions about other forms of religious and religiously related attitudes and behaviors.

What then is the condition of American Catholicism
twenty years after the end of the Vatican Council? If sex
and authority and especially authority about sex are one's
criteria for the health of the Catholic population then the
Catholic Church is in grave crisis. If on the other hand
the principle criterion of health is profound loyalty to the
heritage and to the institution which transmits the heritage

then American Catholicism is in very good condition in the middle 1980s, much better than it was in the late 1950s and early 1960s, precisely because Catholicism has survived a painful crisis of reappraisal and survived that crisis with the loyalty of most of its members unshaken and, perhaps, unshakable.

CHAPTER TWO

The Economic and Educational Context

The years since the end of the Second Vatican Council
have been marked by a profound and accelerating economic and
occupational changes among American Catholics, changes so
massive and so sweeping that no serious reflection on the
condition of American Catholics can afford to forget even
for a moment that the religious change related to the
Second Vatican Council came at the same time that economic
and occupational changes were sweeping American Catholics
ahead of white Protestants' economic achievement. Moreover,
planning for the future of the American Catholic Church must
take into account the fact that economic and occupational
change has not ended and will not end before the beginning
of the next century. It is likely to go on at even more
rapid pace in the next two decades that it did in the past
two decades.

One of the ways to trace the economic history of a population is to investigate the educational and occupational
decisions that young people of a given birth cohort made in
their late teens and early twenties. American Catholics
born in the 1890s had to make a decision about college education and in all probability about their career choice
during the nineteen-teens. The educational achievement and
the occupational category of people born before 1900 is a
pretty good indicator of what the social and cultural envi-

ronment was for American Catholics in the nineteen-teens.
This method may overstate the rate of actual college attendance at that time because some of the respondents born
be-fore 1900 will have made a decision later in life to seek
college education. When one says that in the nineteen-teens
and the nineteen twenties the college attendance rate of
Catholics was .70 of the college attendance rate of
Protestants, one is slightly over-estimating the rate.
Catholics may have been somewhat less than seven-tenths as
likely to go to college as white Protestants in that era.

In the nineteen thirties, forties and fifties, the college attendance rate of Catholics to Protestants was .9. In
the sixties and seventies the Catholic college attendance
rate became slightly higher than that of white Protestants,
approximately 1.1. In the most recent decade, the ratio of
Catholic college attendance to Protestant college attendance surged to 1.43. Catholics who are maturing in the
1980s are half-again as likely to attend college as white
Protestants in the same age cohort. The Catholic "catch up"
was achieved in the sixties and the seventies and the big
surge ahead is a phenomenon of the present moment.

A similar phenomenon is to be observed about the choice
of professional and managerial careers: in the nineteen-
teens the Catholic rate was .65 to the white Protestant. In

the twenties it went to .81, in the thirties and forties to
.90, in the fifties to 1.07, in the sixties and seventies to
1.10 and in the eighties to 1.50. Catholics are now half
again as likely to choose managerial and professional careers as white Protestants.

Similarly, in the choice of a white collar career (managerial, professional, sales and clerical), the ratio of
Catholics to Protestants making those choices at the first
part of this century was .9, in the thirties, forties, fifties, and sixties it became virtually even (1.00), in the
seventies the Catholic white collar rate was 1.30, and in
the eighties it became 1.60. The generation of young people
attending college, graduating from college, and making career choices at the present, in other words, is half-again
as likely in comparison with Protestants of the same age
level, to choose white collar and professional careers and
to attend college. They represent not the first generation
of American Catholics to achieve parity with white
Protestants but rather the first generation to notably excel
white Protestants in their educational and occupational
achievement It is a generation, American Catholic leaders
should realize, that is going to be very different even
from the generation immediately before it.

This educational and occupational achievement is, of course, reflected in the income of American Catholics. In the early 1980s American Catholics made more money by about a thousand dollars a year than white Methodists, three thousand dollars a year more than white Lutherans, and five thousand dollars a year more than white Baptists. They however, lagged behind white Presbyterians by three thousand dollars, white Episcopalians by eight thousand dollars and Jews by ten thousand dollars.

Irish Catholics, the first of the major immigrant groups, add a thousand dollars to each of the statements in the previous sentence about Catholics. Only Jews and Episcopalians make more money in contemporary America than do Irish Catholics. Italian Catholics are only a thousand dollars a year behind Presbyterians in their annual income (Catholic annual income as calculated in the NORC General Social Survey in the early eighties is twenty-six thousand dollars, Irish Catholics, thirty thousand dollars, Italian Catholics, twenty-eight thousand six hundred dollars).

These income statistics, however, include all American Catholics of all ages and hence the older generation of American Catholics who were part of the generation that reached educational parity with their white Protestant counterparts. If one looks at Catholics under forty, those who

were most likely to benefit from the surge in economic and
occupational achievement in the last twenty years, one finds
that Catholics earn two thousand dollars more than
Episcopalians and a thousand dollars more than Presbyterians
and have become the most affluent gentile religious group in
America.

Not only Irish Catholics, but Italian and Polish
Catholics under forty now earn more money than do white
Presbyterians and white Episcopalians. Indeed, under forty
Italian Catholics have passed the Irish in income and earn a
thousand dollars more a year on the average than do their
Irish Catholic counterparts. There is no reason to think
that, with their greatly increased educational achievement
and occupational prestige, these three Catholic ethnic
groups, trailing only the Jews in income, will not continue
to be the most affluent ethnic groups in America and more
affluent than those two mostly upper-class and upper-middle-
class Protestant denominations, the Presbyterians and the
Episcopalians.

When the Second Vatican Council, began Catholics had
achieved rough equality with white Protestants. Twenty
years later they have achieved economic and occupational superiority. Parish priests facing a typical Catholic congre-
gation on Sunday must realize that they are now preaching

to a group which is or is about to become, with the exception of the Jews, the most affluent denominational group in American society.

Moreover, Catholics are now to be found in large numbers at the very top end of the educational bracket -- those who have achieved graduate degrees. During the last twenty years American Catholics have become between a fifth and a quarter of the professorate. There are approximately as many Catholic university faculty members as there are Jewish university faculty members; whatever may have been true of the past, there is no longer any obstacle in the Catholic culture preventing young Catholics from pursuing academic or intellectual or artistic careers and from being as successful as anyone else is in these careers.

At one time it might have been true that Catholics sacrificed the intellectual life to achieve financial affluence. The evidence that this is no longer the case, however, is now overwhelming. Two Canadian scholars reviewing the several decades of discussion about American Catholics and the intellectual life concluded that there was absolutely no reason to assume any more that Catholicism was a barrier to intellectual success. Catholics are to be found now in the most distinguished universities in the country and indeed to be achieving excellence and eminence in these universities.

The two Canadians also added that this transformation in the intellectual life of American Catholics has not been reflected either in the Catholic universities, which still tend to be poor, or in the administration of the Catholic Church which still tends to ignore the skills acquired by considerable numbers of its membership in graduate programs, especially in the arts and sciences. Not only must the American Church for the remainder of the present century deal with a much more affluent and much better educated population, it must also deal with an ever-increasing intelligentsia, composed of men and women with the best professional or academic credentials that can be acquired in American society.

Lip service is frequently paid to the notion that American Catholics are changing rapidly, but it is difficult to overestimate the extent of that change or its importance. When the Second Vatican Council began twenty-five percent of the college graduates in the country were Catholic and half of the Catholic population were either immigrants or children of immigrants. Now, twenty years later, Catholics are half-again as likely to attend college as white Protestants (perhaps a little more) and at least as likely as white

Protestants to pursue scholarly or professional careers that require graduate training. The transformation from immigrant to professional upper-middle class for non-Hispanic Catholics has been achieved almost completely in the last twenty years -- an enormous transformation. All the indicators are that the pace and the scope of this transformation will continue and accelerate in the remaining years of the century. Whether it is good or bad to have a well-educated and presumably independent lay population is hardly a matter worth debating; the truth of the matter is that American Catholics have now become well-educated and independent, perhaps better educated and more independent than church leadership realizes.

It is a truism that the priest is no longer the only educated person in his parish. It is almost becoming a truism that in many parishes the priest is one of the least well-educated persons of his own age group. It is not astonishing that this change would produce trouble, friction, conflict. What is surprising is that despite their tremendous economic and educational progress in the last twenty years, ethnics are still Catholics and the defection rate has not changed.

To put it a little differently, those Church leaders who might in some of their darker moments wish that they could get rid of the contentious, opinionated, independent professional-class Catholics who are now becoming typical, are wasting their time. The well-educated Catholic professional is here, he/she is here to stay and is not about to leave the church. But not about to participate in the church on any other terms but his or her own.

CHAPTER THREE

The Political Context

Ever since Catholics began to move to the suburbs after
the Second World War and to achieve economic parity and then
superiority over the white Protestant population, it has
been cheerfully predicted that Catholics would eventually
end their long-term commitment to the Democratic party.
Indeed, in 1970 when John Kenneth Galbraith wrote his famous
article in THE NEW REPUBLIC magazine about the new coalition
that would take control of the Democratic party in the seventies, he left Catholics out, an omission which was confirmed at the Democratic convention of 1972 when two
obviously Catholic political leaders, Richard Daley and
George Meany were expelled from power.

The notion that Catholics would not be Democrats much
longer is very much part of the wisdom of mass media political commentators. There is, however, precious little evidence to support it. Using data from the national election
surveys that have been done since 1952 by the University of
Michigan, one can demonstrate that there was a de-alignment
from the Democratic party (towards "Independents," not towards the Republicans) in the Nixon years which ended in the
middle seventies. (The 1984 Reagan election is excluded from
this analysis because one election does not a trend make.)
The de-alignment was somewhat greater for Catholics than for
Protestants, though only marginally so. In the early fif-

ties a little more than sixty percent of American Catholics describe themselves as Democrats, in the late seventies and early eighties about fifty-five percent described themselves as Democrats.

The decline in Democratic affiliation among American Catholics took place at about the same time, ended at about the same time and involved approximately the same change numerically as did the decline in Catholic Church attendance.

However, this slight change in political affiliation has had little effect on the actual voting behavior of American Catholics. Indeed, American Catholics are somewhat more likely to vote for Democratic senatorial and congressional candidates in the late 1970s and early 1980s than they were in the 1950s. Just as we shall see shortly, the "advantage" of Catholics over Protestants in church attendance continues to exist even in 1980, so also the Catholic "advantage" over Protestants in voting Democrat continues in the 1980s. About three-fifths of the Catholics in the country, regardless of what they say their political affiliation is, routinely vote for Democratic congressional and senatorial candidates.

Finally, the Catholic propensity to vote Democratic in presidential elections has gone through an interesting cycle from the fifties to the eighties with the net result that

the proportion has not changed very much across three decades. About half of American Catholics voted for
Democratic presidential candidates in the fifties and about
half voted for Democratic presidential candidates in the
late seventies and early eighties (for Carter against Ford,
and for Carter against Reagan).

In between, however, the Catholic presidential voting
pattern has fluctuated more than the Protestant voting pattern. The increase in Democratic presidential votes for
Catholics during the Kennedy/Johnson years was greater than
the increase in the Democratic vote among Protestants. The
decline in Catholic votes for Democratic candidates in the
Nixon years was sharper than the decline among Protestants
and the resurgence of the proportion voting Democratic in
the elections was sharper among Protestants than among
Catholics in the Carter campaigns. However, at all times the
proportion voting Democratic in presidential elections was
higher among Catholics than among Protestants. In summary,
Catholics did "de-align" from the Democratic party a little
more abruptly than did Protestants in the late 1960s and
early 1970s; however, this de-alignment does not affect the
proportion of Catholics voting for Democratic senatorial and
congressional candidates. While the Catholic presidential
vote has been more volatile than the Protestant presidential

vote, Catholics are as likely today as they were in the
1950s to vote for Democratic presidential candidates and
still more likely to vote for a Democratic presidential can-
didate than are Protestants.(Protestants in this analysis
include both white and black.)

The statistics I have cited thus far in this chapter
are not a secret. They are available to anyone in the
country through the University of Michigan election research data files. Catholics are still Democrats even
though they were slightly more affected by the dealignment
of the Nixon years than were other Democrats. It is unlikely that these data, repeated again in the present book, are
going to have the slightest effect on the pronouncements of
mass media pundits. For thirty years Catholics have shown
by their votes that the pundits are wrong when they predict
Catholic disenchantment with the Democratic party.

The fiction that Catholics are somehow or the other
more conservative than other Americans and therefore do not
"belong" in the party -- a fiction which surely influenced
Professor Galbraith's article and the behavior of the
McGovernite Democrats at the 1972 convention -- apparently
does not yield to disconfirming data. The myth of the "conservative blue collar hard hat hawkish chauvinist Catholic
ethnic is a matter of religious conviction, one might almost

say of religious prejudice. It cannot be abandoned because
of the personality needs of the people who adhere to it --
including a number of self-professed Catholic "liberals".
However, it must be said once again in this book and for the
record: with the exception of a slight de-alignment during
the Nixon years, the myth of Catholics turning away from the
Democratic party has no basis in fact.

But Catholics are more "conservative," are they not?
They belong in the Republican party even if they don't know
that yet, do they not? Are not Catholics especially likely
to be militant anti-Communists, Hawkish on military matters,
super-patriots in international relations, conservative to
reactionary on the various social welfare programs the
Democratic party has supported since the New Deal and
through the Great Society.

A prominent Catholic journalist said to me while I was
working on this report, "Aren't our people really the same
kind of folks who cheered for Father Coughlan and Senator
Joseph McCarthy?

The answer on all counts is no. The myth of the "conservative" or "reactionary" Catholic says more about the
personality needs and the religious and political biases of
those who subscribe to the myth than it does about the real
condition of the American Catholic population. The data to

refute the myth are as much on the public record as the data
which support the myth of massive Catholic disaffiliation
from Democratic voting behavior. The data are not believed
not because they are unknown, but because they are
unacceptable.

There are, of course, Catholics who are political conservatives, the kind of people who write letters to chancery
offices and subscribe to The Wanderer or The National
Catholic Register. However, on the average American
Catholics are, as Seymour Martin Lipset has recently pointed
out once again, somewhere in the middle of the American
political stream -- not as left-wing or as liberal as blacks
and Jews (who together constitute about eighteen percent of
America) but substantially more liberal on the average than
white American Protestants, who constitute almost two-thirds
of America.

Some of those involved with the bishops' recent pastoral on the American economy suggested in the national media
that the American middle-class is "conservative" or "uncon-
cerned about the poor." One supposes that such a comment
could be made legitimately if the line separating liberals
and conservatives ran in such a way that only about ten percent of Americans would be defined as liberals. But if the
issue is average place on a broad political spectrum, then

the bishops' economic pastoral was preaching to people who were already among the saved.

In NORC's four-decade tradition of research on racial attitudes, American Catholics always moved more rapidly in the direction of pro-integration stances than did white Protestants living in the same region of the country and the same cities in which Catholics are concentrated. Moreover, research on the Vietnam War indicates that Catholics turned against the war before the typical American turned against the war. Finally, research on attitudes towards nuclear weapons has always indicated more concern about these weapons among Catholics than among white Protestant Americans. Most recently there was greater Catholic support for the nuclear freeze (before the bishops' pastoral on the subject) than was to be found among white Protestants.

On virtually every measure of social and political and racial attitudes Catholics occupy a middle position between Jews and Protestants --a little bit left of center as Franklin Roosevelt described his own position long ago. There are, of course, Catholic conservatives who achieve so much attention in the newspapers, in films, and in novels, the kind of stereotypical person who cheers for anti Communist politicians and military leaders at at Holy Name and Knights of Columbus communion breakfasts. However, if

the typical Catholic position is somewhat left of center, it
follows that there is an even larger number of Catholics who
are liberal or very liberal indeed. On most issues there
are numerically (not in percentage terms) more Catholic liberals than there are Jewish liberals. To blind oneself to
this fact, whether one is engaging in non-Catholic anti-
Catholicism or Catholic self-hatred, is to completely misread the political and social map of America.

Thus, fifty-four percent of American Protestants in the
NORC General Social Survey think too little money is spent
improving and protecting the environment, as do sixty-three
percent of American Catholics and seventy-six percent of
American Jews. Fifty-six percent of American Protestants
think that too little money is spent on protecting and improving the nation's health, whereas for Catholics the proportion is sixty-four percent and for Jews, seventy-four
percent. Forty-five percent of American Protestants think
that too little money is being spent on solving the problems
of big cities, as opposed to fifty-five percent of American
Catholics and seventy-six percent of American Jews.
Fifty-two percent of American Protestants think that too
little money is being spent on improving America's educational system, as opposed to fifty-five percent for American
Catholics and seventy-three percent of American Jews. Twenty

five percent of American Protestants think that too little
money is being spent on arms, as opposed to nineteen percent
of American Catholics and eleven percent of American Jews
(twenty-eight percent of Protestants in the General Social
Survey thought too much money was being spent on the military armaments and defense, as against thirty-eight percent
of American Catholics and fifty-nine percent of American
Jews).

In the 1980s when popular opinion had turned against
the death penalty, Catholics were somewhat more likely to
oppose the death penalty (twenty-three percent) than Jews
(nineteen percent), or Protestants (eighteen percent).
Fifty-seven percent of American Protestants favor gun control as opposed to eighty-two percent of American Catholics
and ninety-six percent of American Jews. Catholics are substantially more likely to support the civil liberties of
Communists, Socialists and homosexuals than are on the average American white Protestants.

They are more likely than Protestants, fifty two percent versus thirty-nine percent, to think that the government should help pay for medical care (fifty-six percent for
American Jews) and more likely (thirty-three percent
against twenty-three percent) to think the government should

help improve the standard of living of the poor (twenty-
eight percent for American Jews).

In the 1980s fifty-three percent of American Catholics
would approve an open housing ordinance, an increase of
fourteen percentage points from the beginning of the decade,
whereas forty-two percent of American Protestants would support an open housing law in the 1980s (thirty percent in the
early 1970s). Half of American Catholics live in neighborhoods in which blacks also live -- as opposed to two-fifths
of American Protestants. In the 1970s thirty-seven percent
of American Catholics said they lived in the same block as
blacks, while in the early 1980s that percentage has gone up
to forty-seven percent of those who live in neighborhoods
where blacks live. In the seventies twenty-one percent of
American Catholics had entertained a black in their home, a
proportion which increased in the early eighties to twenty-
eight percent (for Protestants the figures were seventeen
and twenty-five percent); Ninety-six percent of American
Catholics would not object to their children attending an
integrated school, eighty percent would not object to them
attending a school which was half black, fifty-four percent
would not object to a school in which most of the
students were black (for Protestants the proportion is
fifty-two percent and for Jews, forty-two percent).

Nor can it be argued that this attitude towards education is simply a pretense designed to satisfy the survey interviewer, because Catholics reject busing as vigorously as do other Americans, though in truth, the Catholic opposition to busing (seventy-five percent) is less than the Jewish opposition (eighty-eight percent) and the Protestant opposition (eighty-six percent). A little less than half of American blacks also oppose busing.

Whether the American Catholic attitudes on racial integration are a result of political conviction or religious belief or simply living in large urban areas where they are more likely to know blacks is a matter that cannot be answered with the data available. However, it can be said that in general Catholics are more likely to be in harmony with the teachings of their church on racial matters than are Protestants and also a little more than half of American Catholics now live in integrated neighborhoods and accept racially integrated schools and support open housing laws.

The other half of the Catholic population has not been converted, but the point is here as in so many other respects the stereotype of the typical Catholic being conservative is simply not true. The typical Catholic is more likely to support racial integration than the typical

Protestant and in some few issues as likely to support it as
American Jews.

Other studies (the New York Times election study for
example) showed that fifty nine percent of American
Catholics supported the equal rights amendment as opposed to
fifty four percent of American Protestants and eighty
percent of American Jews. In 1982, before the nuclear
weapons pastoral, seventy two percent of Catholics supported
a nuclear freeze as did sixty two percent of American
Protestants and seventy seven percent of American Jews.

The Bishop's pastoral was, appropriately perhaps,
preaching to those who were already on their side.

There are still a great many Catholics who are
conservative on political issues, anti-integrationist on
racial issues and "hawkish" on military issues, but there
are also many, many Catholics who are liberal on political
issues and pro-integrationist. Moreover, the latter group
is larger than the smaller. Through the years since the
Second Vatican Council and the economic breakthrough of the
American Catholic population, the latter group has grown
larger, not smaller. Those who wish to preach to American
Catholics on political or racial matters misread their
audience if they believe they are lecturing a population
which is overwhelmingly opposed to liberal or integrationist

social policies. In fact, the opposite is more likely to be the case with the majority of Catholics.

In summary then, the American Catholic in the last quarter century has become more educated and more affluent; indeed, she/he is now, if she/he is under forty, part of the best educated and most affluent gentile group in America. However, the American Catholic has not because of this occupational and economic change either abandoned his habit of voting for Democratic candidates or abandoned his position somewhat left of center on the American political spectrum. Though they have become affluent, Catholics have not on the average and by and large become either conservative or Republicans. Those who suggest that the "embourgeoisement" of American Catholics means less concern about the poor or the oppressed are, according to the evidence, simply wrong. Some Catholics, many Catholics, too many Catholics are not concerned about the poor or the oppressed. But a very considerable number of American Catholics do have such concerns. There is not the slightest bit of evidence that economic and occupational success and religious change in the last quarter of the century have diminished these concerns.

CHAPTER FOUR

Religious Attitude and Devotion

First of all , the continuities in religious devotion
and behavior that have persisted in the post conciliar
years:

During the late 1960s and early 1970s about fifteen
percent of those who were raised Catholics in the United
States no longer defined themselves as Catholics. The proportion has not changed. Complex mathematical models that
my colleague Michael Hout has constructed indicate that virtually no one has left the Catholic Church in the wake of
the changes that have occurred since the Second Vatican
Council beyond what would have been expected projecting the
preconciliar trends.

Moreover, about twenty-three percent of American
Catholics were in religiously mixed marriages in the time
immediately after the council, and this proportion has not
changed. The reception of Holy Communion between 1963 and
1974 (the last time on which we have data for the whole
Catholic population) doubled from twelve percent to twenty-
five percent. In the early 1960s, about one out of six
weekly Mass attenders also received communion, now one out
of two receive communion. I have heard this latter finding dismissed casually by many on both the left and the
right -- the former saying the reception of communion does
not indicate greater religious fervor, and the latter saying

that most of the people who constitute the increase probably ought to go to confession on Saturday night anyway and should not be admitted to the sacraments because they are probably practicing birth control. But such cavalier dismissal of an enormous change in religious devotion is thoroughly unacceptable. If someone had predicted in the late 1950s that in a very few years half of the Sunday church attenders would be receiving Holy Communion, the prediction would have been thought incredibly optimistic. Few would have expected that any transformation in the practice of the Church could achieve such an astonishing change.

Furthermore, there is no noticeable decline in either religious experience or the frequency of prayer among Catholics in the wake of the Second Vatican Council. On the contrary, there is something of an increase in both measures of religious behavior. In 1972 fifty-two percent of American Catholics said they prayed at least once a day; in 1984 the percentage had increased to sixty-two percent. In 1972 a quarter of American Catholics reported at least one intense religious experience in their life; in 1984 that percentage had increased to thirty-one percent.

The net loss to Catholicism at the present time through religious change -- defectors minus converts -- is about two percent.

There are two ways of leaving a religious affiliation: one is to acquire another religious identification and the other is to simply become religiously a "none" when interviewed by the survey researcher. Two-thirds of those who leave the Catholic Church in America become members of another denomination (more than nine-tenths of them Protestant) and about one-third have no religious affiliation at all. While these two kinds of "de-alignment" from Catholicism may seem to be related -- to acquire another denominational affiliation being one step less drastic than to have no affiliation at all -- in fact they are two different phenomena. Those who disaffiliate to a "none" are apparently strongly influenced by family conflict and by opposition to church authority and teaching; those who join another denomination tend to do so in association with a religious mixed marriage to someone who is a stronger member of their own denomination than the Catholic is of his or her denomination (the same sort of conversion to Catholicism also happens at time of religious mixed marriages).Those who become members of another denomination tend to be reasonably devout members of that denomination. Those who disaffiliate completely engage in almost no religious practice. It is important to emphasize that both these groups have not increased since the time immediately after the Second Vatican Council.

Ninety-six percent of American Catholics believe in God, seventy percent are "certain" that there is life after death. Neither of these percentages haschanged in the slightest since the end of the Vatican Council (indeed, American belief in life after death has not changed since the nineteen thirties). Belief in the literal interpretation of the bible has declined from fifty-five percent to forty-five percent in the early nineteen seventies. Indeed, ALL of the changes attitude on the literal interpretation of the bible in the last fifteen years are to be found among Catholics with no change among Protestants. The Catholic change is to a category of belief about the inspiration of the bible that is certainly doctrinally acceptable to the Catholic heritage: The bible was written by men inspired by God, but it contains some human errors.

In a wide variety then of devotional, doctrinal, and behavioral matters since the end of the Vatican Council there has been no change. In some matters, frequency of prayer and reception of Holy Communion for example, there has actually been an increase of reported religious devotion.

There has been, however, a considerable decline in con-
victions about papal authority. In 1963, before the
council, seventy percent of American Catholics thought that
it was certainly true that Jesus handed over the leadership
of his church to Peter and the popes. Ten years later that
proportion had fallen to forty-two percent and five years
after that it was about the same proportion among young
Catholics. However, in 1974 only thirty-two percent thought
that it was certainly true that the "Pope is infallible when
he speaks on matters of faith and morals," and five years
later only twenty-five percent of young Catholics agreed
with that position. Authority and, as we shall see subsequently, sexuality, but only certain kinds of sexuality and
perhaps only certain kinds of authority, represent the areas
of most notable long-term decline in Catholic attitudes
since the time of the Second Vatican Council.

The most interesting issue and the most complicated
concerning the alleged decline in Catholic fervor since the
Second Vatican Council is Sunday Mass attendance. In the
years immediately after the Council, about two-thirds of
American Catholics went to church every Sunday. Beginning
in 1969, the year after the birth control encyclical (and
four years after the end of the Council), this proportion of
Sunday Mass attendance began to decline precipitously. By

1975 the proportion of Catholics attending Mass every week
hovered around fifty percent. Patently, if that decline
were to have continued, Catholic churches would soon have
been empty on Sunday. But, interestingly enough, the decline stopped in 1975 as suddenly as it had started six
years before. Moreover, at the same time there has been no
change in church attendance among American Protestants.
Indeed, the proportion of American Protestants who in the
annual Gallup survey said they went to church last Sunday
has not changed since 1940 -- the line at forty percent attendance rate stretches straight across the page. Catholic
attendance, twenty-five percentage points or more above the
Protestant attendance, has now fallen to ten percentage
points above the Protestant. However, since the decline
stopped almost ten years ago, now the two church attendance
rates march across the page in parallel lines, closer than
they were in the middle 1960s, but still separate from one
another and not converging.

Looking at the phenomenon from the distance of ten
years, the abrupt stop is even more surprising than its
abrupt start. In two separate and independent surveys, the
same explanation accounted for the change -- a change in attitude among a substantial number of Catholics on sex and on
religious authority. In the 1963/74 Catholic school stud-

ies, the variables were papal infallibility and attitude towards birth control. In the 1972-1984 General Social Survey
the variables were confidence in religious leadership and
attitudes towards premarital sex. In both cases ALL of the
change in Sunday devotion could be accounted for by the parallel change in attitudes towards authority and sexuality.
The change in Catholic Church attendance, therefore, began
four years after then end of the Vatican Council and seems
to be more intimately related to a reaction to the birth
control encyclical in 1968. The decline stopped in 1975 because attitudes on birth control and premarital sex had virtually "bottomed out" among American Catholics. The decline
in church attendance, in other words, began immediately after the birth control encyclical and ended when Catholic
readiness to accept the church's teaching on birth control
and premarital sex reached rock bottom.

It was frequently said when this finding was reported
in Catholic Schools in a Declining Church that a lot of
other things had happened in the church in the sixties besides authority and sex or, alternately, that there were
other problems which faced the church besides authority and
sex. Both these statements are undoubtedly true.
Nonetheless, the other events that happened did not and do
not account so completely and totally for the decline in

church attendance. Moreover, it is doubtful that anything else that has happened in the American Church in the years after the Vatican Council is so important to the intimate lives of so many people as the birth control encyclical.

To deny that the abruptly begun and abruptly ended decline in Catholic religious practice is the result of a violent reaction to the birth control encyclical is to fly in the face of research evidence of such quality and persuasiveness that on any other matter there would be almost no reason for doubt. Leaders and commentators on Catholic life may try to produce other explanations for the decline in church attendance (without any data to support such explanations, of course). They do so at the peril of self-deception, hiding from obvious and overwhelming facts. As I have said repeatedly before in other writings and at the beginning of this book, I do not conclude from the reaction of the Catholic laity to Humanae Vitae that the Pope should not have issued the encyclical. That is a matter of teaching authority and doctrinal belief that is beyond my competence as a sociologist in this context to discuss. I am not reporting what should have happened. I am merely reporting what did happen. Humanae Vitae may have been an absolutely essential and indispensable exercise of papal authority (though it must be noted that Leo XIII in his

encyclical on marriage in the late nineteenth century did
not mention the issue of contraception).

One question remains unanswered: how is it that so
many Catholics did not leave active Catholic practice in the
wake of the birth control encyclical? If two-thirds of the
Catholic population went to church every week in the late
1960s and only fifty percent go every week now but only
about twelve percent accept the birth control teaching, we
have three different groups of Sunday church attenders --
sixteen percentage points who have stopped going to church
because of the birth control encyclical, twelve percentage
points who continue to go to church regularly because they
accept the teaching of the encyclical and, a group larger
than the other two put together, thirty-eight percentage
points who continue to attend church regularly even though
they reject the teaching of the encyclical. How can this
happen? Why does it happen?

To the second question first. As I mentioned earlier,
Michael Hout and I noted that the de-alignment of Catholics
from the Democratic party paralleled in time and to some extent in scope the de-alignment of Catholics from weekly
church attendance. Was there, we wondered more playfully
than realistically, a common link between these two "one
jolt" changes? Much to our surprise, there was. Catholics

who describe themselves as strong Democrats or strong
Republicans are as likely to go to church in the middle
1980s as they were in the late 1960s. One finds an ever
greater proportion of de-alignment from regular church attendance as one departs from the groups with the strongest
political commitment so that the biggest decline in church
attendance between the end of the Vatican Council and the
present is to be found precisely among those who describe
themselves politically as pure Independents.

The increase in the religiously "non-aligned" Catholics
(those who do not attend church regularly) is "accounted
for" by the increase in the politically "non-aligned"
Catholics (those who describe themselves as "Independents")
and vice versa. To dis-affiliate from the party is also to
dis-affiliate from regular church attendance. Professor
Hout and I have a complex mathematical model (the reader is
referred to our article on this subject if he's interested
in the model) which uncovers a "latent structure" pattern in
the data which accounts for both religious decline and political "de-alignment." We call the variable "loyalty",
looking at it from its positive end. It is perhaps a kind
of "ethnic" loyalty which held Catholics in their patterns
of regular church attendance despite the birth control encyclical and in the Democratic party despite the events of

the '68 and '72 Democratic conventions' "reform" of the Democratic party. Such loyalty seems to explain the thirty-eight percentage points of American Catholics who go to church regularly even though they reject the birth control teaching. It is clear on the basis of the research that Professor Hout and I have done that people continue to go to church regularly despite the trauma of the birth control encyclical because of an intense loyalty to their religious heritage, a loyalty that is also connected with their political heritage. How long this loyalty will last is an interesting question. As I will note in subsequent paragraphs, there is no sign at the present that Catholics coming of age in the 1980s are any less loyal to their religious heritage than Catholics who came of age in the '70s, the '60s, the '50s, or even the '40s.

Many Catholics reject the birth control teaching but still attend church and some receive communion every week. It is possible in other words to be a "selective" Catholic or a "do it yourself" Catholic. If loyalty or commitment to one's heritage is the explanation of the motivation, how do these "selective" Catholics (who are almost eighty percent of the regular church attenders) deal with their consciences?

One hypothesis, derived from the religious imagination theory summarized in the first chapter, would be that a positive image of God might account for the ability of the dissidents to harmonize their dissidence with church teaching and regular attendance. Experiencing themselves as "close" to God and being likely to think of God as a "lover," I hypothesized, might cancel out any inconsistency between doctrinal and devotional practices.

The young adult study sponsored by the Knights of Columbus in 1979 provides information on the religious imagination of young Catholics. While there were not enough young respondents who accept the Church's birth control ethic to use that variable in the analysis, twenty-three percent of young Catholic adults thought that a young couple living together before they are married was almost always wrong, while seventy-seven percent thought it was sometimes or never wrong.

There are two different ways that religious imagination variables might function. There might be an "intervening" variable between ethical dissent and church attendance or there might be an interacting variable exercising influence on church attendance only for dissidents.

In the first case, because the dissidents are less likely to think of God as a "lover" and because they are less likely to think of themselves as close to God, they are less likely to go to church. Such an explanation of the different rates of church attendance copes with the problem of how dissidents can attend church regularly by eliminating the problem. Dissidence, as such, does not affect church attendance, save indirectly; in this case, because the dissidents do not have such "positive" religious imaginations. There is a certain amount of improbability in such an explanation, for it seems to eliminate all conflict between an ethical stand on the one hand and devotional behavior on the other. It seems improbable that in the real world there is no tension between the two aspects of Catholic affiliation.

In the second possible explanation, there would be no correlation or very little correlation between the strength of the religious imagination and church attendance for those who are not dissident and a moderate to strong correlation between the imagination and behavior of the dissident. In such a case, there would be no difference in church attendance between dissidents and non-dissidents whose closeness to God and perception of God as a "lover" were high; but as the intensity of the religious imagination diminishes, the intense church attendance will diminish sharply for the dissidents and slightly or not at all for the non dissidents.

Such a possibility seems inherently more attractive as
it suggests that the religious imagination cancels out the
church attendance effect of the dissent for those who have a
strong religious imagination. The latter is a countervaling
force acting against the effect of ethical dissent when dissent is present and having no impact, because an effect is
not required among those who do not dissent.

Closeness to God, in this research, was measured by
asking the respondent to place himself somewhere in a series
of five concentric circles and the image of God as a "lover"
was part of a series of items that the respondent was asked
to rate according to his reaction as to whether he was likely to picture God in such a fashion (some of the other images were "Creator," "Judge," "Master," "Father,"
"Redeemer," and "Mother"). These two items were chosen because one seemed to be a satisfactory indicator of religious
experience and the other a satisfactory indicator of religious imagery and because it was hypothesized that those who
felt close to God and pictured God as a "lover" would be
more likely than others to think that God would be tolerant
of dissent from church teachings. While He/She might not
necessarily approve of dissidence, She/He might nonetheless
be presumed to be rather more pleased with the dissident

being in church regularly than not being there. Those who
are "lovers" normally want to have their beloved around.

Some thirty percent of the Catholic adults were
"extremely likely" to picture God as a "lover," and ninteen
percent placed themselves in the bull's eye of the circle as
"very close" to God.

Both the image of God as "lover," and the experience of
being close to God correlate negatively with dissent from
church teaching; thus, if Catholic leadership wished to diminish sexual permissiveness, it would appear that it would
be wise for them to emphasize strongly the image of God as a
"lover" and the possibility of close personal relationship
with God, a policy that might shock and even be repugnant to
some Catholic leaders, although it is hardly inconsistent
with Catholic teaching.

What is the nature of the relationship between these
two aspects of the religious imagination and church attendance? And is this relationship different for the dissidents and the non-dissidents? Correlation coefficients 1
established that the anticipated interaction does, indeed,
occur. For the dissidents, the correlation between regular
church attendance and a sense of closeness to God is
.32 whereas, for non dissidents, the relationship is zero.
For the former, the correlation between the image of God as

"lover" and church attendance is a significant .19 and for
the latter, a statistically insignificant .08. The
religious imagination, in other words, has no effect on
church attendance of those who accept the church's sexual
ethic, and a considerable influence on church attendance for
those who do not accept the sexual ethic.

Do these correlation coefficients "account" for the
different levels of church attendance and thus adequately
explain why some dissident Catholics still show up at Mass
on Sunday morning (or on Saturday evening) despite their
dissidence? The results of the multiple regression model
show that the first interaction (experience of God) accounts
for half the difference and the second interaction (image of
God) accounts for the other half. Quite simply, some
Catholics who dissent are able to attend church regularly
because the intensity of their religious imagination --
experience and imagery -- cancels out the negative impact of
their ethical dissent, and one need not search any further
for an explanation.

Note, incidentally, the dilemma for Catholic policy
makers involved in this finding. If Catholic leadership
preaches the love of God and chooses to emphasize the
possibility of closeness to God, and thus increases the proportion of young adults who imagine God as a "lover" and ex-

perience a sense of closeness to Him, they will, indeed, facilitate a decline in sexually permissive attitudes. On the other hand, while doing that, they will also increase the probability that those who remain dissident will engage in inconsistent and perhaps ecclesiastically undesirable behavior and become regular church attenders despite their doctrinal differences with the ecclesiastical magisterium.

If it becomes an important policy concern for the Catholic hierarchy to eliminate such inconsistency, they would have to adopt a policy discouraging the imagination of God as a "lover" and a feeling of closeness to God which, again, if the relationships continue to hold, would increase the amount of dissent with official church teaching (a policy change which would assume the bishops would permit themselves to be caught in the awkward position of preaching against closeness to God and against the image of God as "lover").

Young Catholics who have a strong feeling of closeness to God and are extremely likely to imagine God as a "lover" and who also reject the church's sexual teaching are as likely to attend church regularly as their counterpart on the religious imagination measures. Dissidents are less likely to go to church regularly than the non dissidents only at the low end of the religious imagination scale.

Strong imagery of God keeps young Catholics close to their
church even when ethical dissent might otherwise lead them
to lower levels of religious devotion. In the absence of
such strong imagery, dissidence does indeed lead to less intense religious devotion.

Nor does it seem likely that church leadership will
have much effect on their behavior by insisting on the power
of its own authority. Dissidents are significantly less
likely than the non-dissidents to think that it is certainly
true that the pope is infallible and to endure the primacy
of authority of Peter and his successors (20 percent versus
34 percent). It is interesting to note, in passing, that
the overwhelming majority of even the non dissidents do not
strongly endorse these Catholic doctrines that have received
so much emphasis in the last century.

The dissidents who attend church regularly are significantly less likely to pray daily and to pray several times
a week than are the non dissident church attenders, of whom
one-third pray every day and two-thirds pray every week.
There are no significant differences between the two groups
in the frequency of the reception of Holy Communion and activity in parish organizations and reflection on the purpose
of life and the experience of God. It is especially worth
noting that more than one-third of those who reject the

church's teaching on premarital sex receive Holy Communion
as often as they attend church. Their ability to cope with
religious strain is manifest not only in their church
attendance but also in their reception of the Eucharist.
However, the dissidents are neither malcontents nor
anticlerical. They do not differ from the non dissidents
who attend church regularly in their approval of the quality
of preaching, the empathy of their parish priest and their
approval of the way the pope, the bishop and the pastor
perform their jobs. Moreover, they are not significantly
less likely to approve the possibility of their daughter
becoming a nun. Finally, there are no significant differences in the proportions of those who have favorable attitudes toward the church, who talk about religious problems
with the priest, who have read spiritual books recently or
served as lay lectors or ministers at Mass.

They are, however, more likely to have had serious
doubts about their faith and, if they have had these doubts,
also more likely to have resolved them. They are also more
likely to be uncertain about life after death. Religious
dissidents who attend church regularly seem to be young men
and women who have had serious questions about their religion and have resolved these questions in favor of a God of

intimacy and love and against an institutional church that
seeks to impose ethical norms on them.

Church leaders are likely to react with the charge that
such young men and women are hedonists and materialists and
captives of the "contraceptive" mentality, a word that can
be found often in recent papal and hierarchical warnings.
It would appear that there may be some grounds for the
charge of materialism and hedonism. Dissident church attenders are twice as likely to say that they have been drunk
at least once in the last month and that they have been high
on some other kind of drug during the past year. One could
put two interpretations on such behavior: One could say
that the materialistic dissident has not learned that there
are certain kinds of behavior that are incompatible with
ethical religious commitment; or one could say they might
have learned that a loving God might possibly be more tolerant of drink and drugs than some church leaders are.

In the matter of "contraceptive" or "antilife" mentality, the evidence is mixed. Dissidents and non dissidents
do not differ in their thinking about the ideal age of marriage or that the ideal number of children is at least
three. How could anyone say that young people who think
that their ideal to have at least three children are
victims of a "contraceptive" mentality? Nor is there a

significant difference between the two groups in their conviction that the first pregnancy after marriage should come within two years.

However, the dissidents are more likely than the non dissidents to approve legal abortion if there is the possibility of a serious defect in the child or the mother wants no children. Nevertheless, three-quarters of the dissidents disapprove of abortion in the latter case and three-fifths of the non dissidents approve of it in the former case. The majority of regular church attenders who reject premarital sex will nonetheless approve of abortion if there is the possibility of a serious defect of the child and the majority of those who approve of living together before marriage reject legal abortion if the mother merely wants no more children. The link between dissidence and the "contraceptive" mentality is then, it would seem, not absolute.

There are two major and glacial shifts that the data seem to indicate: 1) an appeal from institutional church leadership to God and 2) a conviction that God does not want you to stay away from church because you reject a specific teaching of the church. The devout dissidents are rejecting any claim by the magisterium to have a monopoly on God.

To summarize the argument about Sunday church attendance thus far:

1. The decline in Catholic church attendance began and
ended abruptly. Its beginning can be accounted for in terms
of a violent reaction to the 1968 birth control encyclical,
its ending by the termination of change on birth control
that occurred when virtually everyone had rejected the
official teaching.

2. A large proportion of those who rejected the birth
control teaching nonetheless continued to attend church regularly because of a "loyalty" or "commitment" to the
Catholic tradition, which relates to deeper structures in
their personality and culture that also affect their refusal
to leave the Democratic party under political pressure.

3. This latter group which is now four-fifths of the
regular Sunday church attenders apparently is able to justify its "selective Catholicism" by an appeal to God's love
over institutional church authority. Once more I must insist that I report this appeal and do not necessarily endorse it.

What are the prospects for Catholic devotional behavior
in the years ahead?

The "single jolt" occurred in the late 1960s. Its effect was spent, with the bottoming-out of Catholic sexual

attitudes, in the middle 1970s. There has been no further decline since then. Given the powerful preconscious and un- conscious forces of commitment and loyalty that seem to be at work and the "rationalization/justification" that seems to have justified "selective Catholicism" there is no a pri- ori reason to think that church attendance will begin to de- cline again among American Catholics -- unless one believes that church attendance rates are volatile and that there is a long term tendency towards decline. However, as we have seen from discussion of the church attendance rates of American Protestants, the opposite is the case: church at- tendance rates seem to be very stable over time. There does not appear to be any long-term tendency towards decline. THE ONLY DECLINE IN CHURCH ATTENDANCE IN THE UNITED STATES SINCE 1940 WHEN THE SURVEYS ON SUNDAY CHURCH ATTENDANCE WERE FIRST UNDERTAKEN, HAS BEEN THE SINGLE ONE-SHOT DRAMATIC DECLINE IN CATHOLIC CHURCH ATTENDANCE BETWEEN 1969 AND 1975.

At all other times and for Protestants at all times the church attendance rate has not changed. It has now been ten years since the post-encyclical decline ended and one would speculate not unreasonably that further decline in Catholic church attendance will occur only if there is some similar trauma -- if, for example, the synod of bishops in the autumn of 1985 should require that every Catholic married couple take a public oath that they are not and will not practice birth control (even in the unlikely event that such a policy be adopted, it is not clear that it would be enforceable).

What about young people, it will be asked, is it not true that young Catholics do not go to church very often? As they grow older, will not their low rates of church attendance pull down the average for the Catholic population? Was the cohort that matured during the troubled times of the late sixties less religious than the cohorts that preceded it?

First of all, for all Americans regardless of religion, there is a "life cycle" relationship between age and religious devotion. Forty-five percent of the Catholics in their late-teens (eighteen to twenty) go to church at least two or three times a month. Only thirty-eight percent of Catholics between twenty and thirty go to Mass at least two or three times a month. For people in their thirties and forties the rate goes to fifty-five percent. For people in their fifties, to sixty-five percent, in their sixties, to sixty-nine percent, in their seventies, to sixty-three percent and in their eighties, to sixty-two percent.

If it is true -- as it obviously is -- that church attendance rates are lower among young Catholics today, the question must be asked whether this is merely a life cycle phenomenon or whether it is also a cohort experience. Do those Catholics who were born in the forties and the fifties and the sixties go to church less often, given the impact of the "jolt" of the late sixties and early seventies, merely because they are younger, or in addition to the age factor is there something in their maturational experience that depresses their attendance even lower than it would be for previous cohorts at the same age? On the other hand, are they marching through the life cycle process at about the same rates of church attendance by their predecessors at the same phase of the life cycle?

In technical terms, which can be appropriately used here, the null hypothesis is that cohort -- the years you were born and the years you matured -- does not add to the explanatory power already produced by age: Younger people are marching through their life cycle at approximately the same rates of church attendance as did their predecessors.

Applying a log linear model (for details of which the reader may check the technical paper that Professor Hout and I have written) to the data indicates that, with a few minor quirks taken into account, the null hypothesis cannot be rejected if the dependent variable is church attendance at least two or three times a month.

People in their twenties today go to church less than people who are in their thirties or forties, not because they matured during the troubled times at the end of the sixties and the beginning of the seventies but merely because they are in their twenties. They are not, in other words, an inherently less religious generation than those who went before them but are only passing through an inherently less religious phase of the life life cycle.

If, instead of two or three times a month, the dependent variable is spread out into four categories -- weekly, several times a month, a couple of times a year, and never, two of the age cohorts of young people -- those baby boom children born between 1950 and 1959 -- do differ in their life cycle curve from those older than them and from those younger. However the difference is almost entirely between "several times a month" and "weekly". These two generational groups -- born between 1950 and 1954 and between 1955 and 1959 -- will go through their life cycle with a little less "weekly attendance" and a little more "several times a month" attendance. They are not inherently either unreligious or disloyal. Rather they are, as in so many other matters, somewhat more casual.

Their immediate successors, however, -- those born in the first half of the 1960's and hence coming into adulthood after the Vietnam crisis was over -- have returned to the age curve of the generations born during the 1940's and the 1930's. On the basis of the trends established by their present march through the life cycle process around half of them will be going to church regularly by the time they are in their thirties and forties and almost two-thirds of them will be going to church regularly by the time they are in their fifties and their sixties.

This is a projection, not a prophecy: unless something changes, this is the phenomenon that can be expected in the next twenty years on the basis of the existing trends. The decline in church attendance in the late sixties and early seventies did not disproportionately affect the younger cohort. The crises, religious and political, that shaped its generational experience did not make it any inherently less religious or inherently less Catholic.

Priests with whom I have shared this finding find it hard to accept. There are, they say, so many people not going to church. One of the reasons for this impression, however, may be that the baby boom cohort is so large that its temporary absence from regular church attendance makes an enormous impression even though in fact it is no more likely to be absent from church in similar phases in the life cycle

as is the generation that was born during the Second World
War or during the last years of the Great Depression.

As this very large cohort becomes older and begins to
attend church more regularly, the average church attendance
rate for American Catholics will nudge slowly upward, not
because specific rates have changed at all but because a
large generation has come to the age when it is more inclined to go to church. Hence, one can project that in the
next ten years as a sort of rough rule of thumb the annual
Gallup or NORC data about weekly church attendance for
Catholics will indicate slight increases. If there are
such upturns (a percentage point or two perhaps every five
years) and especially if there are no downturns, one can assume that the projection made in this chapter is valid and
that the baby boom cohort, as it moves into its thirties and
its forties, will become as devout as the cohorts that immediately preceded it.

In summary, the decline in Catholic church attendance
in the years between 1969 and 1975 seems to be a one-of-a-
kind phenomenon, due to a changing sexual ethic among
American Catholics and particularly a reaction to the birth
control encyclical Humanae Vitae. In the middle nineteen-
eighties the majority of church attenders (four-fifths) reject the birth control encyclical and yet continue to

"align" themselves on Sunday because of a loylalty not
unrelated to a loyalty that kept them in the Democratic
party despite the McGovern "reform" of the party in the late
sixties and early seventies. They justify this loyalty to
their faith despite the rejection of Roman teaching by an
appeal to the love of God over against the authority of the
institutional church. The decline in church attendance
seems to be over and the cohorts who matured at the height
of the decline apparently have not been so unduly affected
by it as to be less religious than the cohorts who preceded
them.

How long can this loyalty continue, it might well be
asked. The data which Professor Hout and I have analyzed
includes Catholics who were born as recently as 1966. There
is no evidence that they their life cycle patterns of church
attendance is different from those Catholics who were born
in 1936. What comes after them? We will only know when the
generation after them is old enough to be interviewed by the
survey takers. However, the early teen agers today are
growing up in an era much less troubled religiously and politically than the late sixties and the early seventies.
They are also alleged frequently to be "conservative." One
therefore does not anticipate they will turn more radically

away from the church than their predecessors. Time will
tell.

All that can be said at the present state of our
knowledge about the decline in church attendance between
1969 and 1975 is that it was sharp, it was sudden, it was
related to sexuality, its effect was inhibited by loyalty
and by a certain kind of religious imagery, and it is over.
The bishops assembled in the synod may wonder if anything
can be done to reverse it. A scientist must observe, however, such a vast phenomenon is not likely to be easily re-
versed or easily repeated.

Note: (No attempt is made in this report to comment on
or evaluate the condition of Hispanic Catholics in the
United States because there does not exist adequate survey
data to make any generalizations about the problems, the
possibilities and the promise of the Hispanic contribution
to American Catholicism. If the American Church ever begins
to fund serious social research, the study of Hispanic
Catholics would be one of the high priority items on the
agenda for such research.)

CHAPTER FIVE

Sex and Authority

The most obvious serious problem for American
Catholicism in the years after the Vatican Council is the
decline of support for certain components of its sexual ethic among large numbers of American Catholics. The decline
in church attendance was brief and sharp, but it ended with
half the Catholic population still attending church every
week or virtually every week. The decline of the sexual
ethic, however, has been more dramatic, and it has stopped
only because on some items the response is at rock-bottom --
only about a tenth of American Catholics accept some of the
more controversial components of the church's sexual ethic.

The problem is made more acute because of the fact that
unlike previous times in the church's history, the ecclesiastical institution has chosen to invest heavily its prestige and authority in demanding compliance with sexual
teachings. Thus, the turn against some of the components of
the sexual ethic by American Catholics represents not only a
problem of sexual ethic but also a problem of authority.
However, at the beginning of this chapter it is necessary to
remark that not all of the church's sexual or sexually related teachings have been rejected overwhelmingly and that
not all teaching authority of the institution has been
called into question. Unfortunately, the immediate conclusion of that is hardly likely to be acceptable to those

responsible for protecting the church's Teaching Authority:
the overwhelming majority of American Catholics give the
church's Teaching Authority credibility and consent under
circumstances which they determine, not circumstances which
authority determines.

First of all, we will consider those areas of the sexual ethic where there has been no significant change in the
Catholic position from the beginning of the 1970s when
NORC's General Social Survey was launched. American
Catholics continue to support and by substantial majorities
the church's teaching on extramarital sex and homosexuality
without any significant change between the early 1970s and
the middle 1980s. In 1972 seventy-four percent of American
Catholics thought extramarital sex was always wrong; in
1984, seventy percent think it is always wrong. At the
beginning of the General Social Survey seventy-one percent
of American Catholics thought that homosexuality was always
wrong; in the middle 1980s it is sixty nine percent.   On
both these issues Catholics are somewhat less likely -- by a
matter of a couple of percentage points to condemn
homosexuality and extramarital sexuality than are
Protestants.

Moreover, there has been little change in the Catholic
attitude on abortion since NORC began its annual six item

survey of American abortion attitudes in the early '70s.
American Protestants and American Catholics in overwhelming
majorities (more than nine-tenths) feel that abortion should
be available when the mother's life is in danger or there is
the chance of a seriously handicapped child. On the other
hand, less than half of both denominations believe that
abortion should be available when the mother wants no more
children or approve of abortion on demand. For Protestants
the disapproval was forty-two percent in the early 1970s
and thirty-nine percent at the present, in 1984. For
Catholics the figures were thirty six percent and thirty
nine percent. In other words, the Catholic attitude on
abortion has not changed in the era after the Second Vatican
Council but it is still hard to distinguish the Catholic
attitude towards abortion and the white Protestant attitude
towards abortion. The majority of both groups take
ambivalent positions, approving the availability of abortion
under some circumstances and disapproving of it under other
circumstances. Such ambiguous positions, of course, are
unacceptable to both the pro-life and the pro-choice groups.

On matters of birth control, divorce and premarital
sexuality, however, there has been a drastic decline in
Catholic acceptance of the official teaching of the institutional church. In 1963 over half of the American Catholic

population disapproved of both birth control and divorce.
Now only little more than a tenth believe that remarriage
after divorce is impossible and that birth control is wrong.
Moreover, it would seem from NORC's 1970 study of Catholic
priests that priests anticipated this change of position on
the part of lay people and that the majority of American
priests (perhaps nine-tenths) also do not support either the
birth control or the divorce teaching. The official
position on remarriage after divorce to some extent has been
eased because of the much greater availability of annulments
which, however much the official position may properly deny
it, still seems to most people to be pragmatically Catholic
divorce.

The General Social Survey does not ask questions about
the legitimacy of contraception; however, it does ask whether birth control information should be made available to
high school students. At the beginning of the '70s twenty-
two percent of Protestants and nineteen percent of Catholics
in the country said that such information should not be made
available to high school students(about the same proportion
which thought that artificial birth control was wrong). In
the middle 1980s the proportions had declined to fourteen
percent and thirteen percent. It would therefore appear
that attitudes on the availability of birth control

information for teenagers are fairly good indicator of
attitudes on birth control in general and that the Catholics
continue to reject by a margin of almost nine to one, the
official teaching of the institutional church on birth
control.

If Catholic support for the official teaching on birth
control declined drastically in the 1960s, it was teaching
on premarital sex that declined drastically in the 1970s.
In 1972 a third of American Catholics thought that premarital sex was always wrong. By the middle 1980s only a fifth
(twenty percent) thought that premarital sex was always
wrong. In the same period Protestant opposition to premarital sex declined only five percentage points, from thirty
-nine pecent to thirty-four percent.

Looking at the other end of the scale, percentage
thinking that premarital sex is not wrong at all, the proportion for Protestants increased from the beginning of the
General Social Survey to the present from twenty-five
percent to thirty-six percent and for Catholics from twenty
seven percent fourty-four percent. Thus, almost half the
Catholic adult population thinks that premarital sex is not
wrong at all, a finding which may in its own way be even
more shocking than the rejection of the church's official
position on birth control.

One fact that is obvious from the findings reported
here is that the argument that a changed attitude on birth
control would lead to a changed attitude on abortion and on
homosexuality does not seem to be valid. In the last fifteen to twenty years Catholics have changed radically their
attitudes on birth control, divorce and premarital sex, but
have not changed their attitudes on extramarital sex,
homosexuality or abortion -- though it must be noted that in
some respects their abortion attitudes even at the beginning
of the period being studied were at odds with the position
of the official church. (The New York Times CBS exit poll
of the 1984 election showed that only eight percent of
American Catholics thought that the abortion issue -- raised
so dramatically by the hierarchy in the months before the
election -- was one of the two most important issues that
would affect their voting -- this percentage was lower than
the percentage of Protestants believing that abortion was
one of the two most critical issues in the 1984 election).

It would appear that American Catholics in overwhelming
numbers have decided to reject not only the church's position that sexual pleasures may not be divorced from procreation, but also the church's insistence that sexual pleasure
may not be divorced from the married state (though perhaps
not from the intention to enter the married state).   On

the other hand, the majority of American Catholics do think
that once one is married, sexual pleasure should be limited
to the marriage relationship and that sexual pleasures
between persons of the same sex are not to be approved.
Finally, American Catholics, at least under some
circumstances, agree with the teaching authority of the
church that abortion ought not to be available. However,
they do not accept the official teaching even on abortion.
However, on the question of abortion, unlike the question of
premarital sex and birth control, there has been no change
since the early 1970s.

Can anything be done to recall the Catholic laity to
the official sexual ethic? It must be said that at the
present time it does not appear that the mere repetition of
the official position by church leadership has any effect on
Catholic attitudes and behaviors. Thus, if one measures
Catholic attitudes on premarital sex, abortion and birth
control at the time the Pope came to the United States and
began to insist vigorously on the traditional doctrine, and
the present time, one can find no change at all in the direction desired by the Holy See. In 1980 twenty-three percent of American Catholics thought that premarital sex was
always wrong; in 1984 it was twenty-one percent. In 1980
sixteen percent of American Catholics thought that abortion

ought not to be available even when a woman's health was in
danger; in 1984 the percentage was fourteen. In 1980 twenty
percent of American Catholics thought that birth control
information ought not to be made available to teenagers and
in 1984 the proportion was thirteen percent.

Moreover, even on those issues which the majority of
Catholics agreed with institutional authority, the papal
campaign to recall erring members to the official doctrine
does not seem to have had impact. Thus, in 1980 seventy
percent of American Catholics thought that extramarital sex
was wrong; in 1984 it was 68%. In 1980 seventy-one percent
disapproved of homosexuality; in 1984 it was 69%. In 1980
sixty-six percent rejected abortion on demand and four years
later 62% rejected abortion on demand. On most of the
items, in other words, there is a slight though not statistically significant decline in Catholic acceptance of the
official teaching despite the very considerable emphasis the
Pope and the Vatican and the American hierarchy have put on
these issues. Thus, it does not appear that the mere repetition of the official doctrine has much effect, a truth
which perhaps the leadership of the American Church knows
but which it dare not admit. On the contrary if it there
is any change in the last four years, the change is in the
opposite direction from that which is desired.

Can anything be done to force American Catholics back into line? Perhaps some draconian measure as, for example, insisting that married lay people take solemn and public pledges not to practice birth control or to accept the official birth control position might be effective. However, even such vigorous measures might not be successful. First of all, it is not clear how the married lay people could be constrained into situations where they would have to take such pledges, and secondly it is not at all clear that American clergy, which as vigorously rejects the official position as does the American laity, would be willing to enforce such a program should it be adopted. Moreover, finally, it is not clear that the Holy See itself would readily proceed with such a challenging policy. Short of such draconian measures, however, it does not seem that there is any technique available at the present by which American Catholics can be persuaded once again that birth control, which they do not think is wrong and premarital sex which they also generally do not think is wrong, are in fact wrong and become sins which must be confessed. This point is important: American Catholics are not engaging in actions which they take to be sinful and defying the church by sinning against the church's commands. Rather, they are saying that the institutional church is wrong about such matters. Birth control and premarital sex are not sinful. Obviously, at other times and in other places in the history of Catholicism there have also been such wide-scale rejections of the official teaching. However, certainly never in the history of American Catholicism, have so many Catholics in such apparent good faith decided that they can reject the official teaching of the church as to what is sexually sinful and what is not, and to do so while continuing the regular practice of Catholicism and even continuing the description of themselves as good, strong, solid Catholics.

Need I say it again? I report this phenomenon as a fact and not as something of which I approve.

Any serious discussion of the condition of American Catholics after the Vatican Council must consider the extraordinary situation in which the papacy and the hierarchy on the one hand and the clergy and the laity on the other are in diametric disagreement about what constitutes sexual sin.

To what extent is this situation a result of the Second Vatican Council? The Vatican Council, of course, did not address itself to the issue of birth control, Pope Paul VI having removed the issue from consideration himself and assigned it to his birth control commission. The evidence available indicates that American Catholics switched from

rhythm to the birth control pill as the principal means of
contraception while the council was in session. Did they do
so BECAUSE the council was in session and because they anticipated a change? Such questions are unfortunately unanswerable at the present time (though in principle research
could be done to answer them).

By the time the birth control encyclical was issued,
the laity in very large numbers had made up their mind that
the birth control pill was acceptable. From having accepted
the pill it was but a step to accept other forms of birth
control when the church renewed its ban not merely on the
pill but on all forms of birth control. At the present time
it would seem that the most popular form of contraception
for Catholics, as for other Americans, is sterilization --
an action which the official church would find especially
reprehensible because it is a form of "self-mutilation."

It may well be that the Second Vatican Council changed
the orientation of Catholic laity and clergy towards ecclesiastical authority so that when a particular ecclesiastical
teaching seemed wrong-headed and unacceptable, the clergy
and the laity would reject it no matter how vigorously the
hierarchy and the papacy insisted upon it. Would the same
reaction have occurred if it had not been for the council?
The question is obviously unanswerable. One suspects, how-

ever, that given the increased educational and economic achievement of American Catholics, independence would have asserted itself in any event and that therefore the Vatican Council may have been nothing more than a facilitating cause in this revolution of American Catholics against the official sexual ethic and that this revolution would have occurred in any event. However, such matters are speculative. The fact is that in the years after the Vatican Council and perhaps to some extent influenced by conciliar euphoria and the feeling that change was in the air, American Catholics did indeed rejected some critical components of the official sexual teaching of the church and have done so, as far as one can tell from the present data, irrevocably.

Given the fact that the Holy See has made sexual morality and especially birth control the primary indicator of loyalty to the teaching authority of the church, the crisis created by this rejection is acute. However, it does not seem that it is a crisis that will be easily resolved. The decline in church attendance which appears to have occurred at the beginning of the crisis, has ended. But neither does there seem to be any hint of an increase in the willingness of the laity to acquiesce in the Pope's insistence on a return to the more traditional sexual ethic.

It is beyond the scope of sociological report to make any recommendations as to what might be an appropriate policy decision at the present time. In the conclusion of this book I will offer some tentative suggestions about possible resolution of the crisis, suggestions which I have no hope at all will be taken seriously by anyone in ecclesiastical authority.

Has the institutional leadership of the church, then, lost all authority? Having staked the game, so to speak, on its credibility as a sexual teacher, is the teaching authority of the church now for all practical purposes impotent, unable to command the assent of most of its laity (and most of its clergy) in the United States and also to prevent those who dissent from considering themselves to be and acting like devout and loyal Roman Catholics?

Is it true then that no one listens to the pope or the bishops anymore when they talk about ethical matters?

The truth is far more complex. Sometimes the laity listen and listen very carefully to what ecclesiastical leadership says. Perhaps the most notable example of this was the lay response to the pastoral letter of the American Bishops on nuclear weapons in 1983. In the winter of 1983 before the document was officially released, thirty-four percent of American Catholics and thirty-four percent of

American Protestants thought too much money was being spent
on arms and weapons and defense. A year later in the winter
of 1984, after the pastoral, the same proportion of
Protestants (thirty-four percent) thought too much money was
being spent on defense; however, the Catholic proportion
critical of defense expenditures had risen to fifty- four
percent -- a change of twenty percentage points --
equivalently a change in the minds of some ten million
American Catholics. Devoid of credibility in sexual ethics,
the American hierarchy turns out to have enormous
credibility on matters of nuclear policy, probably more
credibility than they themselves thought they possessed and
certainly more than most outside observers would have
anticipated. In fact, it may well be said that the
effective leadership of the American bishops on the nuclear
weapons question represents a power and an influence of
leadership which does not seem to be matched anywhere in the
world.

It is worth noting, by the way, that Catholics have
tended to be more skeptical of arms expenditures than
Protestants. In the early 1970s, as reported earlier,
thirty-nine percent of American Catholics thought too much
money was being spent as opposed to thirty percent of
American Protestants. It was thus only in the beginning

years of the Reagan administration with a slight increase in
Protestant opposition to defense spending and a slight
decrease in Catholic opposition to it that the Protestant
and Catholic positions converged at a third of both groups
opposing the defense budget. So, in a certain sense, the
bishops were calling the Catholic population back to a
position which had more Catholic support in years gone by
than it did have Protestant's support. But even if almost
two-fifths of Catholics thought that there was too much
money being spent on defense in the early seventies, this is
substantially smaller than the fifty-four percent who
thought the same thing in the 1980s precisely at a time when
there was no change at all in the Protestant attitude
towards defense spending.

Who were the Catholics that were influenced by the pastoral letter?

First of all, it made no difference what the attitudes
of Catholics were on birth control or abortion or
extramarital sex, those who supported abortion on demand for
example, were as likely as those who opposed it to have been
influenced by the nuclear pastoral. Moreover, it does not
seem to be the case that preaching on the pastoral (to the
extent that it occurred at all in parish churches) had any
effect on the change of mind for those who did not go to

church regularly were as likely to change their position on nuclear weapons as those who went every week. Nor does strength of identification with the church have any effect at all on response to the nuclear pastoral.

Who then were those most likely to be influenced by the pastoral? They were to be found in three population groups -- Democrats, self-described liberals, and voters who chose John Anderson or Jimmy Carter instead of Ronald Reagan in 1980. In the year 1983 with the spread of the nuclear freeze movement and a general growing concern about the nuclear arms race in the United States and indeed in the rest of the world, there seems to have been a considerable unease among a segment of the American population, particularly those who for one reason or another were ill at ease with President Reagan and his defense policy. It would appear that the American bishops provided Catholics with this orientation with a focus for their concern which was not provided by any parallel agency or institution for American Protestants. Moreover, one suspects that the effective teaching of the nuclear pastoral occurred in the first week or two after its publication -- when American Catholics heard about it on the radio, saw brief clips on television, read about it in their daily newspapers and (perhaps especially) in the columns of such news magazines as Time and _Newsweek_ and also perhaps heard some of the bishops on the pastoral committee in such programs as the Today Show. Bishops then, if they are to teach effectively at all in the contemporary world, it would appear have to be able to confine their effective message to such intermediaries as magazines, radio, television and newspapers for that seems to be the only way they have access to most of their communicants.

Moreover, it would also seem that bishops greatest impact as teachers will occur when the situation seems to be especially ripe for their teaching. Perhaps accidentally the hierarchy chose to speak out on the subject of nuclear weapons just at the time when American Catholics were especially disposed to hear them -- even before the nuclear pastoral, Catholics were more likely to favor a nuclear freeze than were white Protestants.

It may be that church leadership has mixed feelings about the enormous response to the nuclear pastoral. If you can influence people's attitudes towards nuclear weapons so dramatically, why can't you influence their attitudes towards sex? -- such is a question which Rome might legitimately pose to American bishops. Okay, the Pope might say, the nuclear pastoral had enormous impact. Now go write a pastoral on birth control that will have the same impact.

On the basis of the data considered in this chapter, however, it is very unlikely that the bishops will succeed at a teaching at which the Pope himself does not appear to have enjoyed much success among American Catholics. As humiliating as it may be to church leadership, it would seem that they have influence on their people only when their people decide to permit them to have such influence. The authority of the government apparently rests on the consent of the governed, not only in civil matters of the United States but also in Catholic ecclesiastical matters.

The fact that church leadership has spent a tremendous amount of time and energy teaching propositions to which its laity simply does not listen has not diminished its capacity to have enormous effect when the laity does choose to listen. The prestige and the power and the influence of the bishops then, is not exhausted when it is applied to matters concerning which the laity have no intention to listen. You can spend your authority on sexual matters for years and still have an enormous reservoir -- apparently undiminished -- that is available when you speak on nuclear weapons. Minimally it has to be said that the prestige and influence and power of the ecclesiastical teaching authority of the American hierarchy are sometimes considerable and do not seem to have suffered at least on specific issues in the slightest since the Second Vatican Council. Bishops are very powerful and influential men -- under some circumstances.

When? It is to be feared when the laity decide that the bishops know what they are talking about. There are probably no teachers in the world with more potential power than American Catholic bishops -- an extraordinary statement which I will confess I never thought I would make. However, this extraordinary power cannot be transferred from one issue to another and it exists only when the laity and the hierarchy, through chance or design, are in effective communication with one another. At the risk of being tedious, I repeat what I have said before: I do not necessarily approve of the situation, I merely report it.

The Catholic bishops, as they prepare for the synod in the fall of 1985 at least can be confident of one point: their power as teachers may be limited by the consent of their laity; however, it is still under some circumstances enormous power, like no other power in the world.

Perhaps this is another manifestation -- on the more positive side -- of the loyalty described in a previous chapter. Catholics take their bishops very seriously because of their intense loyalty to the Catholic community. It may well be that the loyalty which keeps Catholics in

their church as active, practicing communicants despite the
fact that they do not accept the church's birth control
teaching also makes them take their bishops seriously as
teachers at least in those circumstances when they think the
bishops' teaching exercise is appropriate.

For those bishops who would demand as right total credibility, this will scarcely be any consolation. For those
who fear, in their darker moments, they have no credibility
at all, this should be considerable consolation.

CHAPTER SIX

The Survival of Mary

One of the more interesting phenomenon of continuity among American Catholics in the years since the Second Vatican Council has been the persistence of the importance of the Mary image in the religious imagination of Catholics. Young Catholics who were studied in the 1979 Knights of Columbus study of Catholics between 15 and 30 had strong and influential images of Mary. This Mary image persists, despite the fact that, in a "liberal" victory, Mary was deprived of her own separate document at the Second Vatican Council, despite the fact that many in the Catholic elite find Mary an embarrassing ecumenical encumbrance, and finally despite the fact that formal devotions to and sermons about Mary seem to have declined in the American church. The survival of Mary is an interesting example of the strange blend of change and stability, continuity and discontinuity that marks the post-conciliar world and of the mixture of practices and attitudes that may seem to make no a priori theological sense.

However, if one approaches religious behavior from the point of view of the sociology of the religious imagination, the persistence of the power of the Mary image despite rejection of the church's sexual ethic, makes a great deal of sociological sense even if it seems theologically inconsistent.

More than seventy-five percent of the young adults said they were "extremely" likely to think of Mary as "warm" or as "patient" or as "comforting" or as "gentle"; sixty-five percent of the respondents checked all four words as "extremely likely," while fifty percent rated Jesus as high on all four images.

Nor were the Mary images irrelevant. Our "madonna scale" (one point for each of the four words checked as "extremely likely") correlated positively with social commitment, frequency of prayer, concern for racial justice and sexual fulfillment in marriage. Mary is not only still fashionable, but, it seems, also still "relevant."

How can this be, one is asked. Have not the Catholic schools deemphasized Mary? Has not the church played down the doctrine in a quest for ecumenical understanding? Is not much of the old-fashioned Marian piety outdated and unappealing?

To begin with, there is no correlation between number of years of Catholic schooling and the madonna scale (or years of C.C.D., either). Secondly, we are not dealing with religious doctrines. Thirdly, however outdated the "lovely lady dressed in blue" piety of the past may be, it was and is peripheral to the attractiveness of Mary as, to use John Shea's words, a "Story of God."

1. The madonna scale would correlate with positive experiences with motherhood as a child.

2. It would also correlate with positive experiences with a spouse, particularly in the most intimate aspect of the relationship -- "sexual fulfillment," as our questionnaire called it.

3. Positive experiences of motherhood as a child would further correlate with sexual fulfillment in marriage and be channeled through (in whole or in part) the madonna image.

4. The madonna image would correlate at a much higher level with personal prayer than would doctrinal orthodoxy.

5. Arguing from history and from anecdotal evidence, we expected Hispanics and Poles to have the highest scores of any Catholic ethnic group on the madonna scale. Our "maternity" measure was composed of four items: a description of mother's approach to religion as "joyous," frequent Communion on the part of the mother, mother involved at least as an equal in family decision making and mother reported to have a strong religious effect on respondents. Sexual fulfillment was one of a list of dimensions of marital satisfaction ranked from "excellent" to "poor." The doctrinal orthodoxy scale was composed of such matters as papal infallibility, papal primacy, mortally sinful obliga-

tion to attend Mass every week, existence of the devil and of hell.

The first four hypotheses were all true at a statistically significant level for both men and women in the United States and Canada (women have higher scores on the madonna scale than men, but there are no important differences in the correlations or any of the other findings).

A positive experience with your mother while growing up leads to a positive experience with your spouse (the relationships are hardly strong enough to be determining). Your image of Mary is the conduit linking these two experiences. Mary connects the story of your childhood with the story of your marriage. Small wonder that she's important.

There is no statistically significant relationship between doctrinal orthodoxy and prayer (in fact, the relationship is 0.07 in the opposite direction). But the madonna scale correlates with frequency of prayer as a 0.37 level, quite high in most social research. Images lead you to prayer, not doctrinal propositions.

On the ethnic group prediction, we were dead wrong, although the hypothesis did not flow from our theory. The Irish are most likely to score high on the scale, "significantly" higher than the rest of the population, perhaps because of their tradition of strong mother figures.

Neither the Jesus nor the God scale correlates with experiences in either family of origin or family of procreation. Mary is the story of God that links the two aspects of "my" story.

She also plays a role in the process by which "my" story and "your" story fuse into "our" story. When husband and wife both are high on the madonna scale, it is half again as likely that they will both say that their sexual fulfillment is excellent (questionnaires were, of course, filled out independently, not that anyone would be likely to conspire on their image of Mary). Furthermore, among those families where both husband and wife are high on the madonna scale, the correlation between one spouse's description of the quality of the sexual relationship in marriage and the other's description of it becomes higher as the years together increase. If we both share a common story of God in the Mary image, we come to share more and more a common story of our own sexual relationship.

Some feminist critics of devotion to Mary have argued that the Mary symbolism traditionally was used to support a "conservative" approach to the role of women, emphasizing fulfillment in the home and family to the exclusion of all else and placing a high value on passivity and fertility. They have also contended that this tradition has "spoiled" the image for contemporary women. We are in no position to discuss the historical impact of Marian imagery on women; however, it does not seem to play any such conservative role for modern young men or women.

There is no difference between those who are high on the image and those who are low in attitudes toward birth control or divorce or abortion in the case of likely handicapped children. They marry at about the same age, have the same number of children, expect the same number of children and have the same estimates of ideal family size (low, but higher than non-Catholics). Nor does a strong Marian image impede college graduation or work after marriage or economic success or propensity to reject the idea that a working mother harms her children.

Those who are high on the madonna scale, however, are more likely to reject abortion on demand and to disapprove of living together before marriage. Only the most rigid ideologue will insist on the "conservative" nature of such responses, especially since the madonna scale also correlates with various measures of social commitment such as concern for the environment and for racial justice and emphasis on social activism as a source of life satisfaction.

Two questions are asked by colleagues with whom we have discussed our findings: Can the young people be fairly said to be "devoted" to Mary, and where did they get the story of God and Mother from if they did not learn it in the schools or C.C.D. class and are not likely to pick it up from Sunday sermons?

We do not know whether our respondents pray to the Virgin, nor do we know whether they are aware of the impact of the Mary story in their lives. We hope in further research to explore both these issues. However, it must be observed that it is the nature of preconscious imagery that it need not be conscious to have an impact, although the impact may be greater if it becomes conscious.

We presume that young people learn about Mary from their mothers. From whom else? We also speculate that they learn it very early in life as they are told the Christmas story. The woman by the crib, they are told, is God's "mommy," a proposition with which the child has no difficulty. Everyone has a mommy, doesn't he? From such an insight it is but a small jump to say that God loves like a mommy. The story is born again.

Our research, however startling, is still preliminary. Much more needs to be done to understand both the role of religious images in the lives of humans and the specific power of Mary. Obviously, Mary is an enormously useful resource for the church. Our teachers and thinkers and lead-

ers, official and unofficial, should make much more of her
than they do. They are wasting an opportunity. The waste
is not going to cause Catholicism to lose the story of Mary.
It's too good to be lost, ever.

We have no way of knowing how non-Catholics in general
react to the Mary symbol. However, we can investigate the
reactions of the non-Catholics who were married to our respondents. Rather surprisingly, Mary's image is almost as
good with them as it is with Catholics: sixty-two percent
say they are "extremely likely" to think of her as "warm,"
sixty seven percent as "gentle," fifty-two percent as
"patient," and fifty-six percent as "comforting."
Two-fifths of the non-Catholic spouses endorse as "extremely
likely" all four items on the madonna scale, not quite as
many as the two-thirds of the Catholic spouses, but still an
astonishingly high number. There is also a correlation even
among non-Catholic spouses between a high "madonna" score
and frequent prayer; fifty-two percent of the spouses high
on the madonna scale pray almost every day, as opposed to
those who are low. (More than half of the Methodists and
Baptists endorse all four madonna items as do thirty-seven
percent of those spouses who report no religious
affiliation.) Mary may actually be an asset to ecumenism
instead of a liability.

In the mind of Church leadership there may be a strong
link between devotion to the Mother of Jesus and sexual "pu-
rity". They would be mistaken, however, to think that this
link is psychologically or sociologically necessary whatever
its theological validity may be. The image of Mary continues
to be enormously important even after some of the key
components of the sexual ethic have been rejected.

The laity, apparently, feel quite at ease not only in
appealing to God from Church leadership but also in appealing to Mary from Church leadership.

CHAPTER SEVEN

Priests

The Catholic laity are surveyed every year in studies
by Gallup and by NORC and every two years in the biennial
Michigan election surveys. The Catholic clergy, however,
have not been studied systematically since the National
Conference of Catholic Bishops Study of the priesthood in
1970. Moreover, because no explicitly Catholic study of the
whole population has been undertaken since the NORC parochial school study in 1974, there is a lack of data about
Catholic attitudes towards their clergy in the years since
then, with the exception of the young adults study in 1979
which provided information about how young Catholics view
their clergy. Thus, one can speak with a good deal more
confidence about the present condition of the Catholic laity
than one can speak about the present condition of the
Catholic clergy. As was remarked in the introduction to
this book, the principal emphasis is on the laity because we
know so much less about the clergy.

Nevertheless, one of the most striking findings of both
the 1974 study of the adult Catholic population and the 1979
study of young Catholics was that priests are still of enormous importance to Catholics. Indeed, the strongest correlate of church attendance and Catholic identification for
both the young people and for the general Catholic population were not issues of sex, birth control, abortion and the

ordination of women. Rather, the strongest predictor of
Catholic behavior and identification was the quality of the
Sunday sermon preached in the respondent's parish church.
Unfortunately for both the clergy and laity, only a fifth of
the Catholic adults in 1974 and only a tenth of the young
adults in 1979 thought that the quality of the Sunday sermon
which they might hear in their parish church was
"excellent." That which is most important among priestly
activities (at least in so far as it relates to the religious behavior of the laity) is also that which priests seem
to do, at least in the judgement of their laity, most
poorly.

In the present chapter I will attempt to pull together
from the 1970 priest study, the 1974 study of Catholic
adults, and the 1979 study of young Catholics some data on
the condition of the clergy, the attitudes of the laity towards the clergy and prospects for future vocations to the
clergy. I wish to emphasize however, that these data are
both sketchy and somewhat out of date, and that they must be
viewed with more caution than data reported in the other
chapters of this study. However, since it is most unlikely
that anyone in the American Catholic Church is going to repeat the mistake the bishops made in the late sixties of
funding a study on the priesthood which produced unpleasant

findings, these inadequate and outdated sources of information are the best that we have available or are likely to have available in the imaginable future.

There were four important findings in the 1970 study of the Catholic priesthood in the United States which, in retrospect, ought to have created considerable concern in the leadership of the American Church about the future of the priesthood:

1. Between a sixth and a fifth of those who were still active in the priesthood were planning, with varying degrees of certainty, to leave the priesthood.

2. More than four-fifths of the Catholic clergy would not insist on acceptance of the official birth control teaching in the confessional. This represented a change from even five years previously before the birth control encyclical and probably an even greater change from ten years before the 1970 study. Few, if any, Catholic priests in 1960 would have been willing to give absolution to penitents who refused to accede to the birth control teaching.

3. Catholic priests were much less likely in 1970 than they remembered themselves in 1965 to engage in active recruiting of young men to be priests like themselves.

4. The occupational satisfaction of associate pastors is no higher than that of semi skilled workers.

When these three findings are combined they point to a loss of nerve, a loss of discipline, a loss of sense of identity in the priesthood, and a decline of job satisfaction among younger priests. When any professional group loses interest in recruiting replacements, that professional group is in considerable trouble. Moreover, when in addition to this loss of interest in recruiting replacements, a substantial proportion of the group is planning to withdraw from the group and those who remain are not satisfied with their work and are unwilling to accept one of the major rules which is supposed to govern the activity of the group, then clearly that particular collectivity of human beings has very serious internal problems.

Unfortunately, the concern of bishops in reaction to the findings of the 1970 study of the priesthood tended, understandably perhaps, to focus on the embarrassment of the discovery that priests had rejected the teaching of the birth control encyclical and the further embarrassment that four-fifths of the priests in the country believed that married men should be ordained priests and that priests who had left the active ministry to marry should be permitted to return (though only two-fifths of the inactive priests actually wanted to return to the ministry and only about one-fifth to the kinds of work that they had been doing before they left the ministry).

Such findings understandably attracted considerable attention from the mass media and put the bishops who had funded the research in an awkward position. How were they to explain to Rome that they had funded research which showed that the American clergy were in fundamental dissent from the Holy See on the question of mandatory celibacy, the return to the active ministry of married priests, and the birth control teaching. It is to be feared that the bishops were so interested in distancing themselves from the project that they missed the underlying warnings that were more serious and more threatening to the effective ministry of the priesthood than the findings on married clergy, celibacy and birth control.

The only practical result of the study was that a committee was set up in the National Conference of Catholic Bishops to worry about the problems of the priesthood, a committee who's impact on the lives and ministry of priests in the United States seems to have been practically nonexistent.

Therefore the identity crisis, the loss of nerve, in the priesthood which was clearly indicated in the 1970 study and which ought to have served as a warning to bishops and

priests alike that there were greater problems ahead for
the priesthood simply were overlooked.

All other problems of the priesthood would be unimportant if the recruiting of young men to serve in the priesthood in years to come was proceeding successfully. However
there is no reason to believe that the reluctance of priests
to recruit men to assist them and replace them noted in the
1970 study has changed in the slightest. Moreover, the 1979
study of young Catholics proved beyond any reasonable doubt
that there were two important persons in the process by
which a young man begins to think seriously of becoming a
priest -- the young man's mother and the parish priest. The
study of Catholic adults in 1974 showed that there had been
a decline of ten percentage points in the number of
Catholics who said they would be proud to have their son a
priest -- though still half the American Catholics said they
would be proud of a son priest and in the 1979 study of
young Catholics indicates that young Catholics also would be
proud to have a son priest in about the same proportions.
However, pride in a priestly vocation in the family is one
thing and active recruiting of young men to the priesthood
either by a parent or by a priest is something quite
different. Approximately five percent of the young Catholic
men in the country had seriously considered a vocation to

the priesthood and another quarter in 1979 had at least given it some thought. The analytic models developed in the young Catholic study suggested that the principal missing ingredient was the absence of encouragement from the mother and the parish priest in pursuing the thought of the vocation. A related important factor was the fear of the commitment to priestly celibacy. If either the celibacy rule was changed OR there was more encouragement for priestly vocations from priests themselves and from the families of young men, there is every reason to believe that the present crisis in vocations would be speedily eliminated.

The numerical decline of the priesthood, which may be the most serious problem facing the church in the wake of the Second Vatican Council, does not seem to be properly attributable to a spiritual decline among young Catholics, a very considerable proportion of whom are interested in social and religious problems and even (ten percent) would be willing to consider a life of dedication to the church. A change in the requirement of priestly celibacy would probably lead to the ordination of fifteen hundred more priests a year than are presently being ordained and a modification of the requirement of the priesthood in which priests would continue to be celibate but would be permitted to serve in

the active ministry for limited periods of time would produce a thousand more priests a year.

Note that most of the benefit in increased vocations
that could be achieved by eliminating the celibacy requirement could also be achieved by the much less drastic change
of permitting limited term service in the priesthood.
However, the most serious obstacle to increasing the number
of priestly vocations still seems to be the lack of encouragement which young men ought to receive from priests
themselves. The celibacy rule is not likely to be changed.
If the notion of a limited service priesthood is not to be
taken seriously, then the principal obstacle to the recruitment of priests is the lack of enthusiasm for such recruitment among priests themselves. As my colleagues and I have
remarked in our report on the 1979 study: In the absence of
more enthusiasm for vocations in the priesthood, the problem
of diminishing numbers of priests will be insoluble.

One sometimes has the impression that some priests refuse to actively recruit young men to the priesthood because
they believe that they can thus force the Church to change
the celibacy rule. It would appear that for many other
priests, their uncertainty about their own vocation and
about the future of the ministry of the priesthood is now
virtually an insurmountable barrier to enthusiasm for re-

cruiting other young men to follow them into the priesthood.

The vocation problem, in other words, is a priest problem and not a young person problem. Paradoxically, it would appear that precisely at a time when the preaching and counselling abilities of priests are most important to Catholics, priests themselves have relatively little regard for the importance of their own work.Though American Catholics may complain about the quality of preaching and the quality of counselling and sensitivity they encounter in the rectory, they still have considerable respect for the sincerity and the diligence, if not the professional competence, of their priests. While many of them, and among the young adults most of them, think that priests are too authoritarian and still expect the laity to be followers rather than colleagues or leaders and while about half of them objected to priests becoming too involved in politics, the admiration and respect and affection for parish priests was still high. Moreover, the most powerful single influence in facilitating the return of someone to the church who had drifted away -- particularly a young Catholic in early and middle twenties -- was a relationship with a priest.

Preaching, counselling, close relationships with young adults, are at least as important in the church of the late

seventies and of the early eighties as they were in the
church before the Vatican Council. And yet, the overwhelming majority of young Catholics have no contact with and indeed no opportunity to establish contact with priests.
Priests, in other words, are at least as important in the
lives of the lay people as they used to be. But unfortunately, perhaps because of poor communication with lay people, they do not seem to have as much confidence in the
importance of their own ministry as they had in the years
before the Second Vatican Council. And because of that lack
of conviction of their own importance and of the future
importance of their work, they are disinclined to invite
other young men to follow them into the priesthood. The
decline is not in the importance of priestly ministry but
rather, it would seem, in priestly perception of the importance of their own ministry. On the basis of the somewhat meager data available to us it is reasonable to
speculate that the clergy continue to have an enormous crisis of morale, a crisis created by the change in the Vatican
Council, aggravated perhaps by the euphoria and then disil-
lusionment in the five years after the council and made
still worse by the defection from the active ministry of between a fifth and a quarter of the priests in the country,
and made yet worse by the conviction, not supported by

facts, that the work of the priesthood is no longer important to the religious life of the laity.

Precisely at a time when the quality of Sunday preaching is a powerful predictor both of the strength of religious affiliation and of the development of the religious imagination, and when contact with the priest is the most important element in a young persons drift back to the church after he or she has drifted away, precisely at this point it would seem, priests are at least as important in the lives of the lay people as they used to be.

The American delegates to the synod of bishops might well say that the crisis among the clergy is acute and demands immediate response, whereas the crisis among the laity does not seem acute and does not require immediate response. The laity are not about to leave the church. The clergy, however, are in the process of committing collective suicide because they do not have enough confidence in themselves and their work to actively recruit young men to follow them into the priesthood.

The laity, for their part, are much more likely to accept changes in the priesthood than is ecclesiastical authority. In 1974 -- eleven years ago -- seventy percent of the Catholic population would accept a married priesthood and fifty percent approved of a married priesthood. For young Catholics five years later that proportion was even higher. Interestingly enough, there is a strong correlation between willingness to consider a vocation to the priesthood among young adults and antagonistic attitudes towards the church's sexual teaching. Many young Catholics consider an "updating" of the sexual teaching as an essential part of a program to attract more vocations to the priesthood. At first glance there seems to be no connection between sexual ethics and priestly vocation, but perhaps the connection is that the sexual teaching of the church, thought by the young adults to be outmoded and inappropriate, gives the institutional church and the priesthood an image which is not likely to make religious or priestly vocations appealing.

The most intriguing finding concerning the priesthood in the study of young adults was the importance of the confidant relationship between a priest and a woman in the life of a married woman and her husband. A confidant relationship with a priest correlated with sexual fulfillment in marriage for the women who were in such relationships and also for the men who's wives were in a confidant relationship with a priest. Furthermore, both the women in such relationships and their husbands were more likely to believe than other young adults in both ecclesiastical celibacy AND the ordination of women. The majority of confidant wives

and their husbands supported the ordination of women (as opposing the minority of the non-confidant women and their
husbands) and the majority of confidant wives and their husbands also supported the continuation of ecclesiastical celibacy. One might conclude from this finding that perhaps
preconsciously those in confidant families understand that
it is precisely celibacy that makes the confidant relationship profitable for a woman and for her husband and that
they also feel that celibate women priests would facilitate
emotional development in husbands. The confidant findings
are intricate, complex and problematic -- though there can
be little doubt that on the basis of the data there is some
special chemistry at work between priests and married women
that helps both the married women and their husbands to
achieve marital fulfillment (and perhaps helps the priest to
achieve fulfillment in his vocation too). This finding is,
as far as I know, the only empirical confirmation of the
value of celibacy to the Catholic Church. When I first
reported it in my book The Religious Imagination, I urged
strongly that ecclesiastical authority pursue the finding in
greater detail so that an argument in favor of celibacy
other than simply "it's a rule" could be elaborated.
Ecclesiastical leaders, however, were not interested,
frightened perhaps at the implications that there could be
intimate cross-sexual relationships be

tween priests and women that benefitted the sex lives of husbands and wives and presumably also contributed to the happiness of priests. It was the kind of sociological finding which, to the extent that it was understood at all, was viewed as an embarrassment rather than a resource.

One has the impression that in the early seventies the ecclesiastical authorities in Rome and the United States made the decision to "tough out" the crisis in the priesthood and to essentially do nothing either to resolve the loss of nerve and identity among priests, to curtail resignation from the priesthood, to think and rearticulate the reasons for ecclesiastical celibacy or to improve the quality of vocational recruiting or to devise imaginative and creative ways to attract more young men to the priesthood. Perhaps it was felt that attempts in these directions would prove unacceptable to Rome or would require too much effort or would be doomed to failure in the face of the sullen resentment many priests feel towards ecclesiastical authority and towards their own perceived declining status in the church.

It is difficult to find anything in the evidence available to us, either from studies of priests or studies of lay attitudes towards the priesthood, that would justify optimism on the present condition of the Catholic priesthood in

the United States. The laity, for their part, seem con-
vinced that priests are important and are certainly not an-
ti-clerical, but they do not give priests high grades on
professional performance. Priests, for their part, have
lost confidence in their ministry and are not actively involved in recruiting young men to the priesthood. And the
hierarchy finally, for its part, is apparently resigned to a
continuing vocation crisis and is not prepared to experiment
imaginatively either in the recruitment of young men to the
ministry or in changes in the life and work of the priesthood that will make it more attractive to young men. The
priest shortage will have to become far more acute than it
is perceived to be at the present time before any of the
three major actors in shaping the future of the priesthood
become sufficiently concerned to address themselves to the
problem. The full impact of the vocation shortage will only
be perceived in the years ahead when the retirement and
death of those cohorts of priests which are large will leave
the church with substantially fewer priests -- some observers say as many as half of the present number before the end
of the century -- than are presently available. The shortage of priests in the United States is presently a problem
which is discussed but not felt. By the time it is felt --
in the next fifteen or twenty years -- it may well be too

late to discuss it. The priesthood in the United States,
and indeed it would seem in the whole Western world, is in
very serious trouble and no one is prepared to do anything
about it or even engage in serious research and reflection
in response to the crisis in the priesthood.

In truth it must be said that we do not fully understand the origins of the crisis: Why did so many men leave
the priesthood as soon as it became possible for them to
leave and still remain in some fashion in the church? What
was there about the change created in the church by the
Second Vatican Council that created not increased confidence
and self-respect among priests, but rather a deterioration
of confidence and self-esteem? Why is it that at a time
when all the evidence indicates that priests are at least as
important to lay people as they've ever been, priests themselves don't perceive this importance? Why did the changes
in the church, received enthusiastically by most priests,
lead not to an increase in vocational recruiting but to a
decline? What has gone wrong in the Catholic priesthood in
the United States since the Second Vatican Council?

Even stated as simply as that last question, the crisis
in the priesthood remains to a considerable extent
inexplicable. The changes of the Second Vatican Council did
something to the priesthood from which it has yet to

recover. Until we understand better than we do now why the council was such a savage blow to the morale, the self-esteem, the self-confidence and the self-respect of priests, we will have to accept as almost inevitable the continued decline in the number of priests available to minister to the church and the mounting problems for laity and for priests because of that decline.

It must be said in all candor by way of conclusion to this chapter that just as the hierarchy of the Catholic Church seems to have lost its ability to influence the attitudes and behavior of its laity on matters of sexual ethic so it also seems to have lost its ability to influence its clergy on matters of self-respect, self-confidence, professional performance and recruitment of priests for the future.

CHAPTER EIGHT

The Catholic Schools

There is no phenomenon more paradoxical in Catholicism since the council than the Catholic schools. On the one hand, the evidence is overwhelming that the schools are remarkably successful both religiously and academically. On the other hand, enrollment in the schools is diminishing and Catholic leadership does not appear to be as committed to Catholic schools as it was before the Vatican Council.

At the time of the 1979 study of young adults eighty-eight percent of the respondents between 18 and 30 had some kind of Catholic education: sixty-four percent of these had attended Catholic grade schools for a time, thirty-six percent had attended Catholic grade schools for all of their elementary education, more than a third of those who did not spend all their years in Catholic schools had at least four years of religious instruction. On the other hand, fifty percent of the young adults surveyed received no religious instruction in high school. Of the other fifty percent, twenty-five percent attended Catholic high schools and twenty five percent attended C.C.D. Seventeen percent of the Catholics during their high school years had four years of Catholic high schools, only eight percent had four years of C.C.D. Seventy-three percent of those who attended public schools at least some of the time said there were years when they did not receive religious instruction. The reasons given, and they add up to more than a hundred because the respondent was permitted many different reasons: twenty-six percent said poor teaching, forty-five percent no interest in religion, eleven percent friends weren't going, thirteen percent said there were no classes offered, fourteen percent said parents did not care, and eleven percent said they already knew enough religion.

So one can conclude that the church gets some instruction to most of its young members, a lot to elementary school children and much less to high school children. However, poor teaching and the unavailability of religious education classes accounts for about only one-third of the non-attendance at high school religious education classes. Thus, despite the plea of C.C.D.'s supporters that if there were more classes and better teaching they would attract more of the "uneducated" young Catholics, the major reasons for young people who do not attend Catholic schools also not seeking religious education are a lack of interest in religion and a lack of support from their parents or friends for religious education classes.

Catholic school attendance had a statistically significant impact on the religious behavior of young people: Forty-three percent of those who had more than eight years of Catholic school attended mass every week as opposed to thirty-two percent who had less, thirty-two percent received communion every week as opposed to seventeen percent, seventy-two percent believed in life after death as opposed to sixty percent, thirteen percent belonged to parish organizations as opposed to five percent, twelve percent had thought seriously of a religious vocation as opposed to six percent, thirty-seven percent had read a Catholic periodical as opposed to twenty-five percent, sixty-four percent were opposed to abortion if no more children were wanted by the mother as opposed to fifty-four percent.

Moreover, these effects of Catholic school education were not merely surrogates for the influence of a religious family or a religious spouse. Among the unmarried young respondents there was a correlation of .11 between family religiousness and a scale that measured religious devotion. The correlation with Catholic schools was .19. Among married respondents the family of origin correlated with

religious devotion .14, the Catholic education, .17 and the
religiousness of one spouse, .21. Thus, the influence of
Catholic school on the religious behavior of young Catholics
is stronger than that of the family of origin and only
slightly less strong than the family of procreation even
when the influence of the other is taken into account.
Thus, the old explanation of the success of Catholic schools
that they were merely duplicating the work of the Catholic
family is simply not valid.

Catholic schools seem to have their effect on those who
attend them, not so much through formal religious instruction class, but rather through the closeness to the Catholic
community which the experience of attending Catholic schools
seems to generate.

Attendance at C.C.D. classes does not have anywhere
near the same effect. Thus, the number of years that one
has attended Catholic schools correlates .25 with the religious devotion scale and the number of years of C.C.D., .02.
The latter is not statistically significant, the former is.
The correlation between Catholic schools and thought of religious vocation is .16. The correlation between C.C.D. and
religious vocation is .04.

correlation between belief in life after death and attendance at Catholic schools is .12, and for C.C.D. .00.
Indeed, there are virtually no statistically significant
correlations between attendance at C.C.D. and later religious beliefs or behaviors and there are strong and statistically significant correlations between attendance at
Catholic schools and adult religious behaviors.

In the three NORC Catholic school studies, 1963, 1974
and 1979 (of young adults), perhaps the most interesting
phenomenon was that in each year the importance of Catholic
schools to the religious behavior of Catholic adults
INCREASED. The correlation between attendance at Catholic
schools and a wide range of measures of adult religious attitudes and behaviors -- church attendance, reception of
communion, attitudes towards vocation, belief in life after
death, activity in parish organizations, closeness to the
church -- increased as the stability of the church decreased. The question asked in the second Catholic school
study (Catholic Schools in a Declining Church) whether
Catholic schools were more important in a time of crisis in
the church than a time of stability has been clearly answered and now twice: Catholic schools are much more

important -- as measured by the strength of correlation between Catholic school attendance and adult behavior -- in a
time of crisis in the church than in a time of stability.

Nevertheless, Catholic school enrollment declines and
confidence in the worth of Catholic schools also seems to
erode.

In the 1974 study it appeared that the decline in
Catholic school attendance was the result of smaller-sized
cohorts coming of school age and the failure to build new
schools in the areas into which Catholics were moving. The
decline in support for Catholic schools thus at that time
seemed to be the result of decisions on the part of school
administrators not to build the schools and not the result
of decision on the part of parents not to use the schools
that were available. It also appeared on the basis of the
1974 study that while Catholic schools were a substantial
extra cost to a parish, most if not all of this extra cost
was absorbed by the larger contributions of parents with
children in the Catholic schools and by the more substantial
contributions to the Sunday collection of parishioners who
had themselves attended Catholic schools. In fact, this
sort of analysis indicated that Catholic schools actually

not only paid for themselves but may even have been a money maker for the parish in that contributions from present and past users of the Catholic schools more than made up for the costs the schools incurred.

However persuasive this argument may have been on paper, it seemed to have had no effect on the decisions of ecclesiastical administrators. For all practical purposes, Catholic school construction has stopped in the last decade. The reasons for the decline of Catholic school instruction even though statistical evidence shows that there is strong support for them and that the schools are more important to the work of the church now than they were before the Vatican Council requires further research to be fully understood. However, the facts are reasonably clear about what has happened to the Catholic schools since the end of the Second Vatican Council. They are as popular as they were, they are more important than they were, and they are in decline, both in numbers of schools and in size of enrollment.

In a previous chapter we observed that there is a life cycle phase in which young people drift away from religious practice, a phase that begins after high school graduation and seems to come to an end when the young person approaches his or her thirtieth birthday. The correlation between Catholic school attendance and return to the church in one's late twenties is .35, a very powerful correlation. there is no correlation at all between attendance at C.C.D. classes and return to frequent religious practice in one's late twenties. Indeed, in some cases the correlation is negative: the more one has attended C.C.D. classes, the less likely one is to return to active religious practice in the late twenties. In all the research we have done on the effects of Catholic schools we have not been able to find any persuasive evidence of ANY effect on adult religious behavior of participation in C.C.D. courses. For all the enthusiasm, for all the energy, for all the financial commitment, it simply has to be said that as of 1979 the Confraternity of Christian Doctrine as a substitute for Catholic schools is simply a waste of time. C.C.D. does not attract a substantial proportion of Catholics -- at least half of Catholics of high school age receive no religious instruction at all, most of them because they don't want to receive religious instruction -- and is not in any meaningful sense an adequate replacement for Catholic schools.

The evidence on this subject is incontrovertible and yet in many if not most parishes founded since the end of the Second Vatican Council the decision has been made that C.C.D. will in fact substitute for Catholic schools. Thus, to evaluate the American Church since the end of the Second Vatican Council one must say candidly that a major change in the post-conciliar years has been to replace Catholic schools in parishes with Confraternity of Christian Doctrine classes, a replacement which has been almost totally ineffective on the religious behavior of the adults who participated in those classes. Moreover, this decision to substitute C.C.D. for Catholic schools has been made in the face of evidence that C.C.D. is not an adequate substitute for Catholic schools. In the post-conciliar church then, ecclesiastical administrators, pastors, educators and bishops have deliberately ignored the evidence of the effectiveness of Catholic schools and the ineffectiveness of the Confraternity of Christian Doctrine and chosen to support C.C.D. as a substitute for and a replacement of the parochial school. It is a decision which is very hard to justify.

Moreover, it also seems that the Catholic schools are the most effective contribution the church is making to the service of the poor, at least that contribution which can most precisely be determined. While Catholic school attendance has been declining, the enrollment of blacks and Hispanics (at least half of the former not Catholic) in Catholic schools has been increasing dramatically. Research done by James Coleman and myself on secondary school students indicates that the Catholic schools have an enormous impact on the sons and daughters of the disadvantaged. Holding constant twelve different parental background variables and academic scores in the sophomore year, the seniors in Catholic schools perform substantially higher on standardized achievement tests than do the seniors in public schools. Moreover, this finding applies not only to Hispanic and to black young men and women but also to white students. The Catholic schools are more effective as secondary educators than public schools for all three racial groups.

But it is especially among the disadvantaged and among the multiply disadvantaged that the impact of Catholic secondary school is likely to be the greatest. Those young

men and women who are disadvantaged by poverty or by low
levels of parental education or by low personal self-esteem
or by having had disciplinary problems when they were soph-
omores or by being on the fringes of the school community or
by low academic scores in their sophomore year are the ones
most likely to benefit from the two years in between sophomore and senior year in Catholic schools. Most of the effectiveness of Catholic schools in dealing with
disadvantaged young men and women can be attributed to the
fact that the schools demand more home work from the students and more advanced course work, especially in mathemat-
ics and English.

Those public schools which demand several hours of home
work a night and more advanced course work have the same effect as do the Catholic schools on disadvantaged young men
and women. But many, indeed most, public schools are not
either able or willing to demand more home work and more advanced course work; the Catholic schools, perhaps because
they have fallen behind the educational fashion, are able to
make such demands and thus able to have remarkable academic
effect on their students, particularly on those students who
come from one or another disadvantaged backgrounds.

Among the many curious paradoxes that affect the present condition of Catholic schools is that in the years since the Second Vatican Council and especially in light of the conciliar document <u>Gaudium et Spes</u> the church has insisted vigorously on its obligations to the poor and on the necessity to exercise the "preferential option for the poor" and at the same time has phased out as quickly as it could much of the most effective service it has ever done for the inner-city poor in the Catholic schools.

It is difficult to think of any other efforts of the Catholic schools in the giant urban centers of America which reach so many of the poor or reach them with such notable effectiveness. Nonetheless, Catholic schools in the inner city are slowly being closed and there seems to be little protest among even those Catholics who are enthusiastically committed to the cause of "justice and peace" and the "preferential option for the poor" to the continuation and reinforcement of Catholic schools. One critic of the bishops' pastoral letter on the economy argued that if the bishops' were serious about serving the cause of the poor, they themselves ought to make a dramatic gesture of such service and one such gesture, according to the critic a very powerful

one, would be to commit themselves to close no more
inner-city schools and also to commit themselves to the construction of more Catholic secondary schools for the poor
and the disadvantaged in the inner cities of the country.

Whether this criticism is valid and whether the policy
recommendation implied in it should be followed is beyond
the scope of the present book. The point, however, is that
the evidence is now completely persuasive that Catholic
schools do indeed render an important service to the poor.
It is odd, to say the least, to see these schools being
closed precisely at a time when the church takes frequent
public stands in favor of the "preferential option to the
poor."

One must conclude this chapter with the observation
that Catholic schools, particularly primary and secondary
schools, are a casualty of the post-conciliar era.
Obviously there was nothing in the documents of the Second
Vatican Council which suggested that the Catholic schools
should be "phased out" and replaced by some form of "religious education" like the Confraternity of Christian
Doctrine program. Nevertheless, in the intellectual and religious climate that developed in the American Church

after the Second Vatican Council, the decision to proceed
away from Catholic schools and in the direction of C.C.D.
was made without the benefit of consultation with the
Catholic laity, serious consideration of the available empirical research, and even public discussion of the reasons
behind the decision. Suddenly the decision had been made:
Catholic schools were out and C.C.D. was in.

The Catholic schools have not been completely closed
down of course, but new ones are rarely built and enrollment
in the old ones is declining as the Catholic population
shifts into the new areas in the suburban fringes of the
large cities of the country. The religious and community
building function of the Catholic school has been sustained
by empirical research beyond any reasonable doubt. The service to the poor function of the school is both self-evident
and has also been sustained by empirical evidence.
Nonetheless, Catholic schools simply are no longer as important to the ecclesiastical institution as they were at the
time of the Vatican Council. Just as there has been a loss
of nerve and confidence in the priesthood despite the fact
that priests are more important rather than less important
than they used to be, so there is a loss of nerve and

of confidence in Catholic schools even though they are now more important both to Catholics and to disadvantaged non-Catholics than they used to be.

There is no research evidence to explain the reason for either of these losses of nerve. Still, the conclusion is inescapable: Catholic schools are a casualty of the era after the Second Vatican Council. They have not disappeared completely but they are in trouble -- and they are in trouble despite the fact that the consumers of Catholic education are for the most part very happy with the product they purchase when they send their young people to parochial schools.

NOTE ON CATHOLIC COLLEGES AND UNIVERSITIES: As it was noted in an earlier chapter, the two Canadian scholars examining the question of the relationship between Catholicism and the intellectual life in the United States concluded that a) there was no conflict between Catholic faith and academic achievement, but b) the institutional church had not caught up with the educational and academic advance of the Catholic population. Most especially the two scholars noted the Catholic colleges and universities had not achieved a quality of intellectual excellence that seems to be

justified by the advanced educational achievement of the
Catholic population.

There is no reason to doubt that Catholic colleges are
presentable undergraduate institutions. In research done in
the late sixties it was clear that the men and women who had
attended Catholic colleges and universities were very loyal
to them, were more likely to want their children to attend
such schools and felt that they had received excellent undergraduate instruction at these institutions. While no new
study of Catholic colleges has been attempted in the last
fifteen years, there is no reason to assume that the situation is any different now. Certainly the young men and women who attend Catholic colleges do very well in graduate
school, in fact better on the average than Catholic students
who attend public institutions, and are successful in their
business and professional careers. However, as centers of
learning, as institutions of research, the Catholic universities are considerably less successful. In a study done by
the Conference Board of Associated Research Councils on the
quality of academic departments at American universities,
Catholic institutions ranked very poorly. Only three
Catholic departments were above the mean on the rating

scores -- two departments of Notre Dame and one at St. Louis University, and all of them just slightly above the mean.

The average ranking of the Catholic graduate departments was substantially below the mean. Indeed, on the average Catholic institutions rated only at the high end of "marginal" in comparison with other universities. None of them rated as adequate or good or excellent or eminent. And some of the Catholic universities were in the bottom sixth of American institutions of higher learning. Despite the "secularization" of ownership and control in the late sixties and the early seventies and despite the serious attempt to enter the higher educational mainstream and despite attempts to modernize and update in line with what was taken to be the spirit of the Second Vatican Council, the Catholic universities are thus far failures as research institutions (with some exceptions in some departments in a few universities) and have not on the average even begun to approach what would be considered presentable mediocrity in the American academic marketplace.

Why this would be so, why the Catholic universities would not be able to take advantage of the increased

economic and educational achievement of the American
Catholic population to achieve at least a little bit of excellence, a small number of quality graduate departments, is
a question that is beyond the scope of the present analysis.

Nonetheless, one must say as one attempts to evaluate
the condition of American Catholicism since the Vatican
Council that there seems to have been very little progress
in updating the effectiveness of the Catholic universities
as research institutions. Moreover, in the late 1950s when
the Catholic Commission on Intellectual and Cultural Affairs
first sounded the toscin against the inferiority of Catholic
universities there was considerable concerned reaction in
the Catholic higher educational institutions in response.
At that time there was little inclination to deny the
charges of Monsignor John Tracy Ellis, Father Gustave
Weigel, and Professor John Donovan that the Catholic higher
educational institutions were not centers of intellectual
excellence. In the early 1980s, however, when the report
cited here was presented, there was almost complete silence
as though acceptance of and resignation to inferiority has
become total.

It would appear that Catholic higher educational institutions at the present time, unlike in the 1950s, are resigned to a permanent condition of inferiority. The director
of the graduate program of the University of Notre Dame, re-
sponding to the findings of the project, said that graduate
programs and research had not been and were not an important
part of the Notre Dame mission and that Notre Dame had no
desire to become a Catholic Harvard. As a statement of
fact, his remarks were undoubtedly accurate. As a statement
of policy and plans for the future, they seem to suggest
that while Notre Dame will continue to call itself a university and continue to justify its existence as a university
because of its graduate programs in the professions -- law,
business and architecture -- in fact, it does not aspire to
excellence in arts and science graduate programs. This, of
course, is a perfectly legitimate decision for a university
to make, but it confirms the impression that the Catholic
universities (of which Notre Dame has the highest average
ranking in graduate programs, followed closely by
Georgetown) do not aspire at the present time to become centers of high quality professional research. That the church

might have need of such centers in the post-conciliar era does not seem to be a factor that influences this decision.

Thus, it must be said in an evaluation of American Catholicism since the Vatican Council that in the last twenty years and despite the enormous change in the economic, educational and academic condition of American Catholics no Catholic university has emerged as even a presentable graduate training and research institution, and at the present time there is no evidence that the Catholic universities see the research function as an important part of a contribution that they should make to the church and to American life.

CHAPTER NINE

The Catholic Family

The most important representative of the church to an
American is that person's spouse. Second in importance to
the spouse is the person's parish priest. The third most
powerful influence on the life of an American Catholic is
that person's parents. Spouse, parish priest and parents --
after those influences, the bishop, the national hierarchy,
the Vatican and the pope trail off, making insignificant and
unimportant contributions to the religious attitude and behavior of the adult Catholic. The church's principal minister, then, to the Catholic lay person is that person's
spouse. Indeed, so influential and so important is the
spouse in shaping the religious response of an adult
Catholic that the church may just as well forget about having any important impact on the person's life unless somehow
or the other the spouse has been enlisted to support what
the church wishes. You either win the spouse as an ally or
the Catholic lay person is simply not going to hear most of
what you have to say. Since, of course, spouses influence
one another, you must win them together. Unless the church
is able to communicate to the family as family, in other
words, its not likely to communicate to them at all.

One hears it said often that "the family" or "the Catho}ic family" is in trouble. But of course there is no such thing as "the family," there are only families and some families have more troubles than others, though no family is immune from trouble.

It is also said that the family is "in transition." Many families are in transition. But the family is a highly flexible and mutable institution. It has always been in transition and it can adapt itself to a wide variety of cultural forms.

If the observation about the family's transitional or troubled status is meant to imply that families are no longer the most important religious influence in a person's life or that the family somehow or the other is going to cease to exist or that most American Catholics are not in healthy and happy family relationships, then the observation is demonstrably false.

The divorce rate among Catholics has increased considerably in the years since the end of the Vatican Council as I reported in the first chapter of this book, from sixteen percent ever divorced or ever married to twenty-four percent. However, this increase in divorce has affected all religious groups in American society and seems to be the result of the combination of fertility control and employment for women. A wife in an unhappy marriage is no longer economically dependent on her husband for the support of herself or her children and thus it is easier financially to terminate a marriage. It is altogether possible that the seeming relaxation of religious "rules" which many Catholics feel has accompanied the Second Vatican Council made it possible for Catholic couples to divorce with somewhat easier consciences than before. That the rate of increase in divorce is virtually the same for Protestants, Catholics and Jews, however, suggests that the factors shaping the rather striking increase in divorce in the 1970s were at work in the whole of American society and not just among Catholics.

If the generally accepted explanations for the increased divorce rate -- better economic security and more effective fertility control for women -- are valid, then the attempts of the church to curtail or diminish the number of divorces among American Catholics through elaborate preparation programs before marriage are doomed to failure. Premarital education is not likely to have much effect on the conditions which drive a woman in particular to end a marriage relationship. Moreover, as was noted earlier, a rise in the divorce rate says nothing about the quality of relationships in couples that do not divorce. It could just as well be the result of the fact that unhappy marriages, indeed, intolerable marriages, are now more easily terminated than they used to be.

In any event, seventy-five percent of the ever married Catholics are still married to their first spouse and while that percentage may diminish in the years ahead (it may also not appreciably diminish because the fertility control and economic security may simply mean that divorces occur earlier in a marriage than previously) the church cannot afford to assume -- as some worried statements from Catholic marriage educators might lead one to believe -- that the family as it has been known among American Catholics in this century is in the process of vanishing.

It is surely true that wives in Catholic marriages are now more likely to work than they were a half century ago. Nonetheless, forty-two percent of mothers in their fifties with their husband present work, forty-seven percent of those in their forties, thirty-seven percent of those in

their thirties, and twenty five percent of those in their
twenties. Even grandmothers today, in other words, tend to
be working mothers. And the change in the proportion of
Catholic mothers who are working mothers since the end of
the Second Vatican Council has not been great -- thirty-
three percent in the early seventies and thirty seven percent at the present time. Forty-two percent of Catholics in
their late twenties say that their mother worked when they
were in grammar school or high school, as do fifty-seven
percent of Catholics in their late teens. Thus the working
wife and mother has been part of the American Catholic scene
for a long time -- at least thirty years and is not the result of the Second Vatican Council.

There is no evidence that marital happiness of husband
or wife is affected by whether the wife works or does not
work. Nor is there any evidence in our research that the
personal happiness of the working wife is greater than that
of the non-working wife, nor is the personal happiness of
the husband greater with a working wife or a non-working
wife. It is very difficult to find any correlation between
growing up in a family where one's mother worked -- even in
infancy -- and the religious devotion, personal life

satisfaction or quality of relationships with one's parent
or remembered quality of relationship between parents. The
only appreciable difference seems to be that the daughters
of working mothers are slightly less likely to feel they
were close to their mother or to feel that they were very
happy growing up. Even among these women, however, there is
skepticism about the charge that a child will be harmed if
mother works. Indeed, the more likely the mother is to have
worked, the less likely young people are to think that the
child will be harmed by a working mother (less than a quarter of Catholics who's mother worked during infancy, childhood, and teenage think the children will be harmed if their
mother works).

Despite the stereotype of the "large" Catholic family,
the young people studied in the 1979 project did not grow up
in families that were significantly larger than other
American families. The average size family for young people
born in the late forties and the early fifties was 3.26 for
Catholics and 3.03 for all Americans. There were, of
course, some large Catholic families but most families were
rather small in size. There has been a sharp decline in
family size in America in the last twenty-five years so that

the young Catholics studied in 1979 expected to have 2.42
children (slightly less than what they thought would have
been the ideal of 2.62 children). This is slightly higher
than the 2.26 expectation of non-Catholics of the same age
cohort. American families, in other words, are smaller by
about one child than they were a quarter of a century ago
and will be even smaller in the years ahead. The Catholic
family was a little bit larger a quarter of a century ago
and is still a little bit larger today (though smaller than
it was a quarter of a century ago). The notion of a drastic
decline in family size, more drastic than is occurring in
the general American population, is based on an erroneous
estimate of the actual size of Catholic families a generation ago. The difference in family size between Catholics
and non-Catholics was not all that great before the Second
Vatican Council and is even less today, but the most notable
change in family size among American Catholics in the years
since the council is not the convergence towards the non-
Catholic mean but, rather, the decline in actual and expected family size which has happened among Catholic families
parallel to all American families. The change, in other

words, seems not to be the result of the Second Vatican
Council -- any more than the large number of working mothers
and the increase in divorces -- but rather the result of
social changes affecting all Americans.

Smaller families, more working mothers, higher divorce
rates -- whether these are pathological or healthy trends
may be a matter of some debate. A hundred and fifty years
ago a family of seven children was required to produce two
adults who would form families of their own. With the decline in infant mortality and maternal death rates, two
children will accomplish a reproduction that seven would
have in what was very recent human history. The woman who
did not work -- on the family farm or store, for example --
was probably more of a rarity in that era than in the present era. The utterly unemployed mother seems to be a historical oddity, a function of the emergence and rapid growth
of the middle class in the North Atlantic countries in the
late 19th and early 20th century. Whether an increase in
divorce rates means anything more than that women (and men)
are able to escape from family relationships that are intolerable may also be a matter of some debate. Perhaps some
divorces are sought frivolously by men and women who could
with effort work out the troubles in their relationships,

however, research that has been done on the divorce increase
since the early 1970s suggests that many of the new divorces
are sought by women who are in not only psychologically but
physically intolerable situations -- victims of frequent
physical abuse for example. Such women seek divorces now
because they are able to afford them and provide for their
children since they are no longer dependent on a husband as
they would have been not so long ago. While one may be
troubled by the increase in divorces and may also suspect
that at least some of the broken homes might have been
salvaged, one can scarcely object if women can escape more
readily now than they could in the past from such difficult
and even dangerous situations.

Might the "Catholic family" be more protected from
these larger social influences which have produced declining
birth rates, rising divorce rates, more working mothers, and
the increase in premarital cohabitation if the Second
Vatican Council had not weakened the barriers separating
American Catholics from the rest of society? Has not one of
the effects of the Second Vatican Council been to make
Catholics "just like everyone else?"

As was noted above, working mothers were a phenomenon
before the Second Vatican Council; it is not clear that
Catholic Americans were immune to other major social and demographic trends before Pope John XXIII convened the Second
Vatican Council. The depressed birth rate of the 1930s, the
inflated birth rate of the 1940s and early 1950s and then
the declining birth rate of the early 1960s all seem to have
affected Catholics as well as non-Catholics, and the tendency towards Catholic convergence with non-Catholics in fertility patterns seems to have been well-established before
the Second Vatican Council. It may be that in the absence
of the "updating" of the council some American Catholics may
have been protected from the increasing divorce rate and the
rising popularity of premarital cohabitation. On the other
hand, the economic and educational success of American
Catholics might have eliminated the protective barriers in
any event. The Catholic divorce rate is still lower than
the Protestant divorce rate (twenty four percent as opposed
to thirty three percent) and premarital cohabitation is less
frequent (or was less frequent in 1979) among Catholics than
among non-Catholics. The Catholic family structure, then,

is still somewhat different from that of other Americans;
while some Catholic values seem to be converging with those
of the rest of the population, other Catholic values are not
in fact converging. The most one can say in a balanced
judgement about the effect of the Second Vatican Council on
these matters is that it may have made some contribution,
probably minor, to accelerating changes that would have occurred in any event and that changing Catholic attitudes on
family, marriage and sex are more the result of energies and
dynamisms at work in the whole North Atlantic world and not
the result of the Second Vatican Council.

The Catholic family structure, however, is still different from a non-Catholic family structure: "power" and
"support" -- those two dimensions of family life on which
researchers concentrate -- are differently distributed in
Catholic families, though apparently more for ethnic than
for religious reasons. Catholic families still seem to have
a stronger concentration of power (especially in parents
over children) than in non-Catholic families, but with the
exception of the Irish Catholic family, there is also more
support between husbands and wives and for children from
parents in Catholic families. Moreover, the Irish

Catholics, whatever their failings are, are still more likely to spend time with their children and to spend time talking to their spouse and even to engage in the hugging and
kissing of children than are other American families. In
general there is more time, more communication, and more
display of affection, as well as more scolding of children
in Catholic families than in non-Catholic families, though
ethnicity is frequently as important as religion (for example the number of hours per week spent with children: Irish
Catholics claim 14 hours, Slavic Catholics 13, Italian
Catholics 12, British Protestants 12, German Catholics 11,
Jews 11, German Protestants 11, and Scandinavian Protestants
10).

These special patterns of family behavior that relate
to religion and ethnicity are not only not unimportant, they
do NOT seem to be diminishing as differences in family size
and some sexual attitudes seem to be diminishing. Research
shows a) that political attitudes and behavior, drinking
attitudes and behavior, attitudes towards aging and dying,
and even religious attitudes and behaviors differ among
relligio-ethnic groups and are transmitted across generational lines even to today's adolescents and b) that

family structure (the blend of "power" and "support") plays
an important part in the socialization process. The more
"Irish" a particular family is, for example, (high on power,
low on support) the more likely its offspring are to engage
in "typically" Irish political behavior -- that is to say to
be politically active. The more Italian a family is, high
on power and high on support, the more likely its offspring
are to engage in typically Italian political behavior (a
non-involvment in politics). Moreover, when young Catholic
married people encounter difficulties in their relationship,
the amount of socialization with family and friends increases, whereas for young non-Catholics the opposite oc-
curs. Finally, Catholics are much more likely to visit with
parents and siblings socially than are Protestants (Italian
Americans are the most likely to visit with both their siblings and their parents, Jewish Americans are second in visiting their parents and Irish Catholic Americans second in
visiting with siblings). These ethnic or religio-ethnic behavior patterns are almost never self-consciously transmitted but absorbed in the early years of childhood and taken
for granted in adult life and are, generally speaking, unaf-
fected by education, by economic achievement, and by

living in "non-ethnic" neighborhoods. In other words, some
aspects of Catholic family life change under the impact of
the influences at work in the larger society and others do
not.

Are Catholic families becoming "just like" other
American families?

The answer is yes and no, yes in some respects, no in
other respects. American society is complex, variegated,
diversified and pluralistic. It tolerates and even encour-
ages a wide variety of different structures of family orga-
nization. Convergence in family size and an increase in
divorce rates does not mean that American family patterns
are becoming homogenous. The a priori assumption that they
are, an assumption one hears not infrequently from Catholic
marriage educators, over-simplifies a much more complex picture. As a rule of thumb it might be suggested that the
more unself-conscious and unreflective a form of family behavior might be and the less likely it is to be subject to
self-conscious reflection and decision making, the more
likely distinctive kinds of behavior are to survive. Church
leaders might be much better advised to study carefully and
empirically the problems and possibilities of Catholic

family life in America before they make their generalizations instead of after they determine policy, if at all.

It might be said, as a hypothesis for further testing,
that the principal effect of the Second Vatican Council on
American Catholic family life is to enhance the possibility
of diversity. The increasing diversification of family
styles among Catholics would have perhaps occurred in any
event given the educational and occupational ability of
American Catholics. The Vatican Council may have added the
extra dimension of greater religious freedom and freedom of
conscience (assumed if not given) in choosing among different kinds of marital and family behaviors.

Nonetheless, if one considers the young Catholic family, married Catholics in their twenties in 1979, one is
struck by how important religion is in their marriage life
-- if not explicitly and self-consciously, nonetheless, effectively and importantly.

The young Catholic family goes through a rather long
and painful period of adjustment for perhaps five or six
years of the first decade of married life. The turning
point is reached towards the end of that first decade and

the marriage survives pretty much on the internal residual strength of the relationship. This crisis is often both religious and sexual. The religious imagery, those cosmic pictures or stories by which people represent and re-articulate to themselves what life in general and their own particular life is all about, seems to be extremely important implicitly if not self-consciously at the critical turning point in the first decade of marriage. The resurgence of the religious imagination in the last three years of the first decade of the typical young Catholic marriage accounts for two-thirds of the rebound from 18 percent to 42 percent of the husbands and wives who both say that the sexual fulfillment in their marriage is excellent. Moreover, the highest levels of sexual fulfillment in marriage are to be found among those young Catholic marriages in which both the husband and the wife have "gracious" religious imaginations (images of God which emphasize the tender and affectionate nature of God's relationship with us) and also both of whom pray frequently (whether together or not, we do not know). Sexual fulfillment, religious imagery, and frequent prayer, in other words, converge especially as young husbands and wives survive the crises of the middle years of the first decade.

Another way of putting the same finding is that at the time of marriage the correlation between the religious imagination of the husband and the religious imagination of the wife is .2, reasonably high -- evidence that people tend to choose as spouses those whose "stories of God" are not unlike their own. By the second half of the first decade of the marriage, particularly if both husband and wife say the sexual fulfillment in their union is "excellent," the correlation is .65. "Your" story and "my" story have converged to become "our" story and marriage seems to have indeed become a "great sacrament," both disclosing to husband and wife through one another God's passionate love for them and also enjoying in the power of God's love a surge of the passion of their own love.

Most of the discussion in this chapter has been addressed to the question of whether the "Catholic family" is becoming "just like any other family." The response has been "in some ways, yes" and "in some ways, no." It is necessary to attempt to answer the question because it is asked so often. A more pertinent question, however, might be whether in Catholic marriages religion plays an important part in binding the husband and wife together. In the conclusion of this chapter we have suggested that even for Catholics who are still in their twenties their religious imagery and their prayer life does indeed play an important part in binding them together. That may be a more important observation about the current condition of American Catholicism in the era after the Vatican Council than the observations about the decrease in family size or the increase in divorce rates. Has religious imagery become more benign and more gracious since the Second Vatican Council and hence does it have even more impact on binding husbands and wives together?

As we shall see subsequently, there is good reason to believe that a notable change in religious sensibility has affected American Catholics in the last twenty-five years and that this change may, perhaps in a convoluted way, be the result of the Second Vatican Council. There is also a hint -- in the present state of our research knowledge, no more than that -- that this change in religious sensibility (which has NOT happened among non-Catholics) has helped to bind together some American Catholics in unions that are both stronger and more satisfying than they otherwise might

be. If such a hint could be confirmed by subsequent re-

search (which of course is not likely to be commissioned)

then it could be said that the Vatican Council has made a

not unimportant improvement to the quality of Catholic fam-

ily life.

CHAPTER TEN

Young People

Older generations assume that younger generations are different -- probably since Adam and Eve complained about the behavior of Cain and Abel. In fact, the differences are often not as great as they might at first seem and the dictum that apples do not fall very far from their trees is often a very good summary of research evidence. Priests, nuns, and parents may well be prepared to insist that the Catholic young people today are "different," not as religious, or not as generous, or not as "Catholic," or not as "loyal," or not "different from others" as they used to be. After all, are they not more likely to use drugs, to engage in premarital sex, to live together before marriage, to refuse to attend church, to reject important Catholic doctrines, and to be critical of and disrespectful towards ecclesiastical authorities?

In fact, a careful consideration of the young Catholics studied in the 1979 project for the Knights of Columbus suggests that the apples are much closer to their trees than many people are prepared to admit. If young Catholics are more likely to engage in premarital sexual intercourse, it can hardly be said that their parents did not engage in premarital behavior that stopped just short of intercourse or that their parents now disapprove strongly of premarital sex. If Catholics in their teens and twenties reject the church's teachings on birth control and divorce, they are not in those respects very different from Catholics over thirty. If their church attendance is not what the church attendance of Catholics was twenty-five years ago, neither is the church attendance of any other age group of Catholics what it was a quarter of a century ago. If the younger generation are committed to "selective Catholicism," how are they different from the rest of the Catholic population? If some of them use marijuana or cocaine, do not many of their parents drink more than they ought to? If they are not at all times devout, socially concerned, responsible Catholic young adults, how many of their parents can be said to be at all times devout, responsible, and socially concerned Catholic older adults?

Have not the changes in the church, both the ones officially approved by the Vatican Council such as the English liturgy, and those unofficially approved by the local clergy, such as "selective Catholicism," weakened the ties of loyalty that bind young people to the church? Has not the experience of growing up in a Catholicism where the "old rules" are not imposed made them somehow less loyal and indeed less Catholic than previous generations have been? In the absence of "Sister's" stern warning and "Father's" drawing the hard canonical line, in the absence of compulsory confession and compulsory Mass and compulsory communion, are not the ties that bind the next generation of Catholic adults to the church substantially weaker than they would have been a generation ago or than they ought to be today? Having lost all the quick and ready answers which religion teachers and parents had before the Second Vatican Council, is not the church now faced with a new generation of young people who don't "know what it means to be Catholic"?

The best answer to all these questions is "no!"

There is nothing in the empirical data available to us to suggest that the generation of Catholics who have grown up since the Second Vatican Council are any less loyal, any less committed, any less devout than their predecessors -- once one takes into account the changes that have occurred in the whole Catholic population that I have reported previously in this book. Granted, for example, the "one shot" decline in church practice in the late sixties and the early seventies, the curve which projects the religious path of young Catholics through the life cycle is no different than the curve for the age cohorts over thirty. When Catholics in their early twenties today are in their early forties, in the beginning of the next millennium, they will be, unless something happens to affect the trends, as likely to attend church weekly as are those in their early forties today. That they would be less likely to attend than Catholics who were in their early forties twenty years ago is a result of the single jolt decline after the birth control encyclical which established a new and lower level of church attendance for Catholics and NOT the result of the younger generation of Catholics being inherently less religious or less loyal to the church than their parents.

Another way of saying the same thing is that the rules and the customs and the regulations and the practices and the styles of the immigrant church are more likely to have been the result of loyalty to the church instead of the cause of it and that loyalty gets transmitted across generational lines by parents and reinforced within generation by spouse, even if "Father" and "Sister" no longer rule with an iron hand, even if indeed they have run away with one another to be married!

Or to say the same thing yet another way, projections based on the available data about Catholic young adults would indicate that as far as the essentials of practice and commitment to Catholicism are concerned, the picture in the first decade of the next millennium will not be greatly different from the picture today -- save presumably that there will be fewer priests and nuns.

Many readers will resist this projection. They will say that my empirical data do not take into account all the energies and forces and factors that are at work. Perhaps they do not. But unless one is to go beyond the boundaries of empirical evidence and make projections by wetting one's finger and holding it up into the wind or investigating the entrails of slain chickens, one must do serious data collection and analysis to confirm that the impressions which contradict the data that I have gathered are correct. Anecdotes about what happened to a family down the street or about what the kids in your parish have done or about your own children or grandchildren are, however interesting and powerful and poignant, no substitute for systematic and disciplined investigation and cautious professional analysis.

It may be argued that the problem will appear not with the generation in its teens and early twenties today but with younger Catholics raised and educated after the rigorous boundaries of the immigrant church had completely disappeared. Such a prophecy may well be correct, but it will nonetheless be prophecy until that still younger generation begins to reach maturity and establish religious patterns of its own. However, the fact that loyalty to Catholicism survives as vigorously among young people in the twenties today as it does in people who are twenty years older indicates that Catholic loyalty has displayed remarkable durability through very trying and difficult times. If it has survived the last twenty years then it may survive a long time to come. How long?

There is no statistical evidence available to answer that question. My instinctive response is to say a LONG time.

There is however, one important difference in the younger generation of Catholics which may well be the result of the Second Vatican Council: younger Catholics, especially those born after 1959, have a sharply different religious "sensibility" than older Catholics, different from those over thirty and forty and even on the average different from those who are just a few years older than them, born in the early and middle 1950s. The younger generation of Catholics, those presently under twenty five, are considerably more likely to picture God as a lover, a spouse, a friend and a mother than are either their non-Catholic counterparts or older Catholics. This religious sensibility correlates positively with frequency of prayer, marital fulfillment, respect for the rights of women, consideration of the possibility of a religious vocation, happiness in marriage, and even disapproval of premarital sex (and negatively while support for premarital sex). The religious imagination as we have said earlier is not a fluffy, pretty, artistic luxury, it is a powerful energy which has considerable impact on the lives of Catholics, a greater impact indeed than does any doctrinal conviction. That more younger Catholics have this "gracious" religious imagination suggests not perhaps a change in the years ahead in the ordinary quantitative measures of religious behavior but a change in the quality of Catholic life as it is lived by at least some members of the present young generation as they move through the life cycle. There is a hint in the data -- at the present it is only a hint -- that this generation may even, precisely because of their more gracious religious imagination, be more likely to attend church and engage in other traditional religious practices as it grows older.

This new religious sensibility seems to be acquired from three different sources -- from a mother (particularly if she went to a Catholic college and is a frequent communicant), from a husband (for women respondents who are married), and from a priest (if one has a close relationship with a priest). As Archbishop Jean Jadot used to remark after being informed of these findings when he was apostolic delegate to the United States, "How else would one expect an ecumenical council to be implemented, through husbands, priests, and mothers!"

The thesis of this chapter bears insistent repeating because it flies in the face of so much conventional wisdom. There is no evidence that Catholics born after 1945 or after 1955 or even after 1960 are inherently less religious than Catholics born during the Second World War or the Great

Depression. Nor is there any evidence that they are inherently any less loyal to the Catholic tradition (which of course is a way of saying that some are more loyal, some are less loyal, but that the average does not seem to have changed greatly) and there are some faint traces of evidence which ought to be pursued in subsequent research that Catholics born after 1960, who certainly have more benign and gracious images of God, may also be more devout, more religious and more loyal than any cohort of Catholics that has been observed in the last fifty years.

Has the Second Vatican Council had serious negative effects on those Catholics who have matured since the end of the council twenty years ago? The most cautious answer available is that the council does not seem to have had any disproportionate negative effect on them. If one concedes for the sake of the argument that the most notable decline in Catholicism we have described thus far in the book -- selective Catholicism (particularly with regard to sex and authority and authority on sex) and decreased church attendance -- have not disproportionately affected young people. These phenomenon are population-wide and have had no greater impact on those who have matured after the council

than they did on those who matured before it.

CHAPTER ELEVEN

Women

Suddenly the Catholic Church discovers it has an enormous "woman problem." In 1974 only twenty-nine percent of American Catholics thought that "it would be a good thing if women were to be ordained as priests," in 1977 that proportion went to thirty-six percent, in 1979 forty percent, in 1982 forty-four percent. Among young Catholics in 1979 the proportion supporting the ordination of women had risen to one half. These statistics suggest a very considerable change in a brief period of time on a subject of considerable importance to church authority and indeed in the teeth of repeated statements from church authority that the ordination of women is an impossibility.

Incidentally, men consistently are more likely to support the ordination of women and Irish Catholics consistently more likely to support it than members of any other ethnic group. At the time of the 1974 NORC study, majority support for the ordination of women was found only among Irish Catholic men over forty-five (a demographic group which perhaps had had considerable experience with authoritative women in the course of its life).

However, the attitude towards the ordination of women is merely one indicator of rapidly changing Catholic

attitudes on the role of women. In the early 1970s sixty-
five percent of American Catholics were likely to reject the
premise that a preschool child is "likely to suffer emotional damage if the mother works." By the middle 1980s that
proportion had risen to seventy-eight percent (seventy three
percent for American Protestants, eighty-seven percent for
American Jews). In the early seventies seventy percent of
American Catholics rejected the notion that woman's place
was essentially in the home. That proportion had risen to
seventy-nine percent in the middle eighties (seventy percent for Protestants, eighty-nine percent for Jews).
Moreover, while in the early seventies two-fifths of
American Catholics agreed that women should leave politics
to men, the proportion by the middle eighties had declined
to thirty-one percent (forty percent for Protestants,
eighteen percent for Jews). As in most other social issues,
then, American Catholics are more "liberal" than the national average, more liberal than American Protestants and only
slightly less liberal than American Jews. In the attitudes
towards the role of women the issue is not Catholics assim-

ilating to a national norm, but rather of Catholics taking
the lead in creating a new national norm.

If these three items are combined into a scale and
those who take the feminist position on all three are defined as "feminist" (a very modest operational definition of
"feminism"), thirty-eight percent of Catholic men could be
called "feminists" in the early 1970s, as opposed to forty-
two percent in the early 1980s, whereas for Catholic women
the percentage rose from forty-one percent in the early seventies to fifty-seven percent in the early eighties. Among
Catholics under twenty the percentage for men is forty-nine
percent and for women fifty-nine percent. Moreover, while
fifty-four percent of the women who do not accept all three
"feminist" items go to church weekly, only 40 percent of the
"feminists" go to church weekly, a statistically significant
difference of fourteen percentage points (there is no difference between "feminists" and "non-feminists" among men).
One may estimate from these data that somewhere between a
million and a million and a half Catholic women do not attend church regularly for reasons associated with these
rather mild "feminist" positions. Moreover, since the

church attendance effect seems to be greater among younger women, the proportion of Catholic women who stay away from church for reasons associated with attitudes on the role of women is likely to INCREASE with the years.

Since forty percent of Catholic "feminist" women still go to church regularly, they apparently finding no inconsistency between their "feminist" commitment and their loyalty to the Church. Who are the most likely to be part of the million to a million and a half whose departure from that loyalty is related to their "feminist" position? Most of the explanation is to be found in experiences in their past. The "angry feminists" are most likely to be college educated, to come from families in which the mother did not work and was religiously devout. "Feminism" has no effect on church attendance if a woman matured in a family where either the mother worked or where the mother was not devout. It would appear that the combination of traditional religion and traditional gender definition has influenced the "feminist woman," especially if she is college educated to view ecclesiastical authority as responsible in part for the problems and frustrations she experiences in trying to break out of the boundaries of traditional gender role definition.

The anger of the "feminist" is rooted more in past experiences than in present experiences but is not thereby any less a problem for the church.

Many of those Catholic women who go to church regularly are also angry (and here the word is not in quotes) but their anger is not sufficiently rooted in past conflicts as to cancel out their loyalty. Rather, they are more likely to stay and complain. In the absence of research on the attitudes of Catholic women -- research which the Bishops Commission during a pastoral on women does not seem inclined to undertake -- the size and shape of the anger of the women who continue to go to church cannot be estimated.

Three influences in the present life of a "feminist" woman from a traditional family background are capable of cancelling out that traditional background so that she goes to church regularly despite her feelings about the relationship between traditional religion and traditional gender role definition: a personal confidant relationship with a priest, a sympathetic and "pro-feminist" husband, and a religious imagination in which there is a propensity to think of God as a lover. A loving husband, a loving God and a sympathetic, if not loving, priest are the principal influences in other words which would cause an "angry" Catholic woman to go to church despite the conflict between her present "feminist" dispositions and the traditional family in which she was raised.

Are these shifting attitudes towards the role of women and the alienation that results from these attitudes a result of the Second Vatican Council? Or is it merely one more phenomenon that has occurred after the council and not because of it?

The Feminist Movement was certainly not caused by the Second Vatican Council. Nor were the social forces that produced "feminism" -- greater education, more employment, more independence for women. "Feminist" attitudes would have spread rapidly in American society if there had never been a Second Vatican Council; it is extremely unlikely given the occupational and educational success of Catholics, men and women alike, that Catholic women (and Catholic men) would have been isolated from the influence of "feminism" if there had not been a Second Vatican Council. Could a case be made that the somewhat greater support for "feminism" among Catholics is a result of the Second Vatican Council?

The only argument that could be used in favor of such a case would be that the euphoria and the chaos created by the Second Vatican Council made it, perhaps paradoxically, easier for Catholics to break with traditional gender models than it was for American Protestants. Certainly there is no empirical evidence to support such an argument and it seems inherently implausible. A more reasonable explanation is that the extra margin of "feminist" support among American Catholics is concentrated in the Irish ethnic group. On the "feminism" scale the Irish are second only to the Jews in support for "feminism" among American religio-ethnic groups -- and considerably higher on the scale than are the other American Catholic ethnic groups. Interestingly, Jewish women are the most "feminist," while Jewish men, Irish Catholic men and Irish Catholic women are all virtually tied for second place. Irish culture has traditionally valued strong and forceful women.

Even today a recent Common Market study shows that on forty-nine measures of Feminism on a survey administered in the nine Common Market countries, the Irish were first or second thirty-eight times (the Danes were in second place in "feminist" responses). Interestingly, Irish "feminists" were publicly outraged about the research findings, insisting that they gave no indication of how bad things actually were for Irish women. The researcher in charge responded by saying that that might very well be true, but they were even worse in the other Common Market countries.

Thus, it is not likely that the basic thrust in the support of Catholic men and women for "feminist" positions is linked to the Second Vatican Council though it may be possible that support for the ordination of women would not have increased so sharply and the issue would not have become such a thorny one so quickly if it had not been for the council and the euphoria about change in the church which the council generated.

Would the anger of Catholic women towards what they perceived to be the church's commitment to the old gender role definitions (of which the "anger" of those "feminists" who do not attend church regularly may only be the tip of the iceberg) have been as great if it had not been for the council and the implicit promise in the council as interpreted by the mass media and as perceived by American Catholics had not hinted at the possibility of greater change in the church than has actually occurred?

Perhaps, though given the social and educational changes among the American Catholic laity and given the large number of Catholic women with occupations and careers before the Second Vatican Council, it does not seem likely that the changes in the church instituted by the council can account for the rise of Catholic "feminism" and for the anger among many American Catholic women at what they perceive as the church's commitment to traditional rigid gender-linked role definitions.

Some religious leaders console themselves with the image of the traditional Catholic wife and mother: strong but obedient, vigorous but docile, dedicated, loyal, devout, transmitting to her children the traditional Catholic religious truths that have been passed on by women like her for centuries, women like their mothers and their sisters, such leaders would like to believe. This is the way, such leaders tell themselves, most Catholic women still are. It is only a handful of nuns or lesbians or radicals who want to be ordained or who want equal power in the church with men.

One suspects that if priests and bishops think that way they have not seriously discussed the issue with their sisters or their mothers. American Catholic women and men have rejected at least in principle and in theory and have rejected by overwhelming majorities the traditional gender role definitions. It may not be at all clear to them what this rejection is going to mean for the future either in their personal or their religious life, but the equality of man and woman in theory and principle at any rate is supported by most Catholic men and women -- and Catholics were more likely to support the late Equal Rights Amendment than the national average.

The "woman problem" then, seems to be not so much the result of the Second Vatican Council, as something that happened after the council, another case of the convergence of religious change with trends of social and economic change which were already at work and which would have had a considerable impact on American Catholicism if it had not been for the council. It may well be that the greater toleration of the parish clergy for such changes, a toleration based on their interpretation of the council's spirit if not the council's letter, has made the "woman problem" less serious for the church rather than more serious. Indeed, it may be that the greater tolerance of the parish clergy for the changing behavior and value patterns of American Catholics has eased many of the acute problems which would have occurred in any case because of the changing social and economic condition of American Catholics.

One has the impression that the leadership of the American hierarchy is now only too well aware that it has a "woman problem" and indeed is juggling its proposed pastoral on women as it would the most sizzling of hot potatoes. One also has the impression that the leadership of the American Church has not prevailed upon the Vatican to believe that the "woman problem" is as serious as they, the American bishops, perceive it to be -- either because they have not argued the case vigorously enough or (as may be more likely) the Vatican hasn't wished to listen carefully enough.

In any event, in this evaluation of American Catholicism since the end of the Second Vatican Council, the point must be made as forcefully as possible: The "woman problem" is serious, very serious indeed. And one cannot imagine a way in which it is not going to get even more serious in the years ahead.

CHAPTER TWELVE

Anti-Catholicism

Has the Second Vatican Council, with its emphasis on ecumenism, produced a climate for religious attitudes in which Catholics have better relationships with Protestants and Jews than they did in the years before the council? Have the statements on religious freedom and on the Jews issued by the council improved the quality of denominational pluralism in American life?

The question is very difficult to answer because most of the research on denominational conflicts done in the last twenty-five years has focused on anti-Semitism. Only one study has been done which investigated anti-Catholicism and its findings, while sparse, are rather chilling. More than one quarter of Americans (thirty percent of Protestants, twenty percent of Jews) agree either that "Catholics are afraid to think for themselves" or "Catholics tend to think the way their bishops and priests want them to think." This view of American Catholics -- patently and blatantly at odds with the reality of American Catholic life -- is especially strong among those who have attended college, who live in the Northeast part of the country and who would describe themselves as "liberal." Indeed, forty percent of liberal, college educated Protestants living in the Northeast section of the country agree with one or the other of those two statements. Anti-Catholicism is surely not as virulent as anti-Semitism, but neither has it gone away and only the most myopic of Catholics believe that the changes since the Second Vatican Council have put an end to nativist bigotry.

The only other data available are from the studies done every four years by the University of Michigan of American presidential politics. In the national samples conducted by the Michigan team, "feeling thermometers" towards many groups in American society were used between 1964 and 1976. On a scale between 0 (cold) and 100 (warm), Americans were asked, where would you place your feelings towards Southerners or liberals or blacks? Or towards Protestants and Catholics and Jews? Three findings emerge from charting the changing attitudes of the three religious denominations towards one another between 1964 and 1976:

1. Catholics have warmer feelings towards both Jews and Protestants than Jews and Protestants have towards Catholics.

2. Jews and Protestants have warmer feelings towards each other than either group does towards Catholics.

3. Between 1972 and 1976 the quality of all inter- religious feelings declined sharply (perhaps in the wake of the Vietnam and Watergate crises). In 1972, for example, 50

percent of American Jews had feelings of over seventy on the thermometer towards Catholics, while 70 percent of Catholics had the same level "warm" feeling towards Jews. In 1976 Jewish feelings of warmth towards Catholics had declined to 32 percent and Catholic feelings of warmth towards Jews to 45 percent. The impressive fact to one who studies the graphs of changing interreligious feelings carefully is that these feelings seem to be rather volatile and to be affected by phenomena in society which have little or nothing to do with religion as such (feelings towards ALL groups in society diminished between 1972 and 1976: interreligious feelings, in other words, were affected by the same kinds of external social forces which affected all intergroup feelings). It is possible that the high point of inter-religious warmth in 1972 was a result of the Second Vatican Council, though that would not explain why Jews and Protestants also had warmer feelings towards one another and why, even though the council ended in 1965, its payoff was not to be found until 1972.

A more likely conclusion, one fears, is that while your relationships among leaders of the various denominational groups have notably improved since the council and while, perhaps, individual Protestants and Catholics and Jews and individual clergy persons relate more warmly, the general attitudes of Americans towards members of other denominations considered as a group instead of as individual persons have not been affected by the Catholic ecumenism of the post-conciliar years.

More important perhaps for evaluating the current condition of American Catholics, Catholics are more likely to have feelings of warmth towards the other religious groups than those other groups are likely to have them towards Catholics. We are the more tolerant ones, they are the less tolerant. Again, the conclusion is inevitable: while anti-Catholicism may not be virulent or dangerous, it has not gone away. Indeed, in so far as our very limited research evidence permits us to say, it has quantitatively been relatively little affected by the Second Vatican Council. When forty percent of liberal college educated Protestants in the Northeastern part of the country still believe (in the early 1980s) that Catholics do not think for themselves, anti-Catholicism is alive and well, and if not potentially dangerous, still a serious problem which the American Church can ill-afford to ignore.

CHAPTER THIRTEEN

Religious Imagination: The Big Change

The most positive effect of the Second Vatican Council
era that social science is able to measure is the change in
the Catholic religious imagination. The "sensibility" of
Catholics has undergone a rather drastic modification in the
last twenty years in the direction of images and pictures
and stories of God which are more benign, more gracious, and
more affectionate.

When this finding is reported there is a tendency for
many church leaders to dismiss it as unimportant. The imagination is something "soft," religious sensibility is something ephemeral and unimportant. What counts in evaluating
post-conciliar Catholicism are "hard," "substantive" issues
of doctrine and morality. The religious imagination may be
all right for children, perhaps even for teenagers, but it
is not especially relevant in judging the religious condition of adults.

Such a response, understandable perhaps in those
trained in the excessively cognitive and rationalist sem-
inaries of the era before 1965, fails to understand that religion exists in experience, imagination and story before it
begins to be articulated in doctrine, catechism, creed, phi-
losophy and theology. Thus, the apostles first of all

experienced the risen Jesus; then they retained those images in their memories encoded in the symbols of their own religious heritage, such as king, lord, prophet, messiah, son of man, son of God, although in applying these images to Jesus, the images themselves were transformed; then they told stories about their experience of Jesus both before and after the resurrection to those whom they wished to follow after them. Only after these three early phases of experience, image and story did primitive doctrine and theological discourse begin to emerge.

Theology developed early; it is certainly to be found in Paul's Epistle to the Thessalonians which was closer to the resurrection of Jesus than we are today to the assassination of John Kennedy. But propositional theology and propositional ethics are the result of reflection on the raw data of religious experience, image and story. Cognitive and ethical theology do not create the religious imagination, they are rather created by it.

The most impressive evidence for this hypothesis is to be found in the correlation between religious imagery (as measured by how respondents rate themselves on four forced choice scales: between mother/father, spouse/master, friend/king, judge/lover) correlate with social and political and marital attitudes and behaviors. Other religious indicators -- church attendance, doctrinal orthodoxy, frequency of prayer, activism in religious organizations, do not correlate at all with, for example, attitudes on race, poverty, nuclear weapons, civil liberties, capital punishment, attitudes towards the equality of women, even sexual fulfillment in marriage. Moreover, on all of these measures the correlation between gracious religious imagery (God as mother/lover/spouse/ friend) and social and political attitudes and behaviors are more powerful for Catholics than for Protestants. The religious imagination seems to have more effect on how people live their lives in this world than any other measure of religion available to us, indeed, of all the other measures of religion put together and to be an even more powerful correlate of how we live and work in this world for Catholics than for Protestants.

Furthermore, for Catholics over fifty there is only a slight difference in their religious images than for Protestants over fifty. Thirty one percent of the Catholics are at the top end of the scale as opposed to twenty-nine percent of Protestants. However, for Catholics in their forties and and under, the difference is much greater --

forty two versus twenty five percent. The former difference
is not statistically significant, the latter is. The difference between Catholics and Protestants in the religious
imagination therefore is concentrated in the younger generation. The Catholic religious imagination changes between
the two age groups from thirty-one percent high on the
scale to forty-two percent high on the scale, while the
Protestant imagination declined slightly from twenty-eight
percent to twenty-six percent. In other words, something
seems to have happened in the last twenty years which notably affected the religious imagination of Catholics in a
more benign and gracious direction but which had no effect
on the religious imagination of Protestants. Catholics in
their forties and under are, to use a different statistical
metric, four-tenths of a standard deviation higher on the
religious imagery scale than Protestants of their age group
and three-tenths of a standard deviation higher than
Catholics over fifty. Something enormous, almost incred-
ible, has happened to the religious imagery of Catholics
since the end of the Great Depression. It is difficult to
think of what else this might be besides the Second Vatican
Council. Catholics, in other words, now have higher scores
on measures which correlate with a wide range of social,

of social, political and interpersonal behaviors. The correlations are even stronger for Catholics than for
Protestants. One therefore can expect a gradual shift in
the Catholic population in the direction of greater concerns
about peace and justice and interpersonal intimacy.

The bad news, then, is Catholics no longer accept one
of the major components of the church's sexual ethic and refuse to listen to ecclesiastical authority when it speaks on
those areas of sexual ethic. The good news is that the
Catholic religious imagination has shifted drastically in
the direction of gracious and benign images and stories of
God, images and stories which have a profound influence on
how people live their lives and are likely to have an even
more profound influence in the years to come.

There are a number of possible reactions among which
one is, "Who cares how they imagine God, they're still practicing birth control, aren't they?" and another is, "Who
cares whether they are practicing birth control, they are
now more likely to imagine God as a lover, a mother, a
spouse and a friend, aren't they? And don't these images
affect almost everything else in their life?"

Deciding which reaction is the more appropriate is beyond the scope of this book.

Are the two phenomena connected? There would seem at
least to be a possibility. As indicated in a previous chapter, it is precisely a benign and gracious image of God
which seems to make it possible for Catholics to continue to
attend mass and receive the sacraments even though they are
rejecting the church's teaching on birth control (and more
recently premarital sex).

In the concluding chapter of this book I will sketch
out a scenario, speculative and undocumented (but document-
able), that might explain these twin critical effects of the
Vatican Council era. For the moment it suffices to say that
ecclesiastical authority, as was noted in an earlier chapter, is faced with an awkward dilemma. On the one hand, if
it tolerates the change in Catholic religious sensibility it
will continue to have selective Catholicism, for the more
Catholics imagine God as a mother, lover, spouse and friend,
the more likely they are to make their appeal to God over
the heads of institutional church leaders. On the other
hand, how can church leadership try to persuade its people
that God is not loving and affectionate, gentle and tender,
passionately concerned about his creatures, when that seems
to be the way Jesus described God? Moreover, changes in religious sensibility, especially of the size described in

this chapter, are not easily undone. If ecclesiastical authority is looking for a policy to compel Catholics once again to accept the birth control teaching, the only obvious policy -- to anticipate the following chapter -- is to insist once more with all the vigor at its command that God is a judge, a master, a king, a father, and that he will punish the "terrible sin of birth control" by sending most of the current American Catholic population to hell for all eternity.

But does ecclesiastical authority seriously want to pursue such a strategy? Moreover, if it should attempt to pursue such a policy, will it be believed? It is very difficult to persuade people that ecclesiastical authority knows more about their own personal experiences of God than they do. There is no reason to suppose that should ecclesiastical authority pursue a policy of emphasizing once again sin, judgement and damnation, the lay people will listen to authority any more than they listens to it when it condemns birth control and premarital sex. Finally, there is no reason to believe either that the lower clergy would cooperate in such a return to hell-fire and brimstone. Thus, it may well be that the institutional leadership of the church is faced with a situation about which it can do very little:

do very little: in the United States in the era after the
Vatican Council, if not exactly as a result of the Council,
there is more love of God among American Catholics and also
more determination to make their own choices on certain ethical issues. More love and more freedom: the two may not
necessarily be linked but in the present condition of
American Catholicism the link between them seems to be irre-
versible. The bishops assembled to the synod in Rome and
the American hierarchy after their delegation returns from
the synod will have a difficult time of it. If they attempt
to persuade the Pope and their fellow bishops that there is
anything they can do to reverse the trend away from the rejection of some elements of the church's sexual ethic and
towards more intimate images and stories of God (and towards
greater concern for justice and peace which are results of
those images) they simply will not be telling the truth.

CHAPTER FOURTEEN

Conclusion

The principal themes of this book can be summed up under five headings:

1. In the years since the Vatican Council American Catholics have surged ahead of their white Protestant counterparts on almost every available measure of educational and occupational and economic achievement. However, they continue to occupy on most issues a place on the left of center of the American political spectrum, notably more likely because of the bishops' pastoral letter to be concerned about nuclear weapons than their Protestant counterparts, likely now by a majority to support open housing legislation and also likely if they live in cities to live in neighborhoods where there is at least some racial integration -- and to accept that integration.

2. There was a sudden and sharp decline in church attendance among American Catholics after the birth control encyclical so that between 1969 and 1975, the proportion Catholics going to Mass almost every week fell from two-thirds to one-half. The entire change could be accounted for by a simultaneous change in attitudes towards some of the church's sexual ethic -- most notably those parts of the church's sexual teachings which deal with birth control and premarital sex. This decline in church

attendance stopped in 1975 and has not resumed, in part because there has been a "bottoming out" effect with regard to
sexual teaching. The percentages accepting the church's
doctrine now are so low that it would be difficult for them
to go much lower.

3. Almost four-fifths of the weekly church attenders
(and at least as large a portion of the weekly communion re-
ceivers) do not accept the church's official sexual teaching. They remain in the church nonetheless because of a
"latent structure" which also accounts for their remaining
in the Democratic party, a latent structure which Professor
Hout and I have chosen to call "loyalty." Church attendance
did not change between '69 and '75 for those Catholics who
at both points in time described themselves as "strong"
Democrats or "strong" Republicans and the most likely change
was to occur among those who moved from being strong
Republican or strong Democrat or even from being Republican
or Democrat to being "Independent." Political de-alignment
and religious de-alignment were not merely linked in the
late sixties and early seventies, they were virtually the
same phenomenon. Those who chose to remain practicing
Catholics even though they did not accept the church's birth
control teaching apparently have been able to quiet their

conscience by an appeal from the institutional leadership to God, from a leadership perceived as harsh, to a God perceived as loving. They have been facilitated in this appeal by the support of most of their parish clergy.

4. The "loyalty" which holds American Catholics in their church does not seem to be diminishing with the younger generation. If one projects a trend line for those born between 1960 and 1966, measured once in their teens and once in the early twenties, that trend line indicates that when they are in their early forties they will be as likely to go to church regularly as the generation born thirty years before them. There is not, as far as church attendance goes, a cohort effect which would distinguish those who were born between 1931 and 1935 from those who were born between 1961 and 1965. Religious styles may very well be different and the younger generation may have very different images of God, but they will be no more de-aligned from the church in their forties than those who are thirty years older than they are.

5. The most obvious positive gain from the Second Vatican Council is a deepened and a more self-conscious loyalty to the Catholic heritage and tradition rooted in richer and warmer experiences, images, and stories of God.

Loyalty and faith as a result of rejection of official church teaching?

Possibly.

Church leaders are not going to like it that I have raised such a possibility, not even as a hypothesis for testing. Candidly, however, I know of no other hypothesis that fits the data quite so well and would cheerfully test any alternative plausible hypothesis should anyone suggest one to me. Ecclesiastical leaders should be willing at least to entertain the possibility that the laity in the experience of turning their backs on the leadership, aided and abetted by their clergy, paradoxically emerged with greater loyalty to the church, if not to the leadership, and a deeper awareness of and sensitivity to the forgiving love of God.

Talk about drawing straight with crooked lines!

The fertility research done by the University of Michigan and the University of Princeton, in the years immediately before the Vatican Council indicated that most American Catholics came eventually to practice birth control. They felt, rightly or wrongly, that they had to choose between their sex life which was essential to keep their marriage together and the teaching of their church. There were a number of different compromises effected that enabled them to stay in their marriage and to stay in the church (note well the stubborn adherence of the Catholic married people to their institution even though the institution, as they perceived it, was putting them in an anguished and painful position). Some, not many, stopped going to church; others went to church but stopped receiving the sacraments; still others confessed birth control, promised to try not to practice it and then received Holy Communion in more or less good faith -- knowing full well that they were not going to run the risk of another pregnancy. A few, with sympathetic confessors, found awkward paths out of the problem, for example they were told if one partner insisted on marital sex that was contraceptive, the other partner might passively accept such marital sex, which passive acceptance did not necessarily mean that the accepting partner could feel no pleasure. Such ethical legerdemain caused considerable amusement among some of the clergy who offered it as advice in the confessional, realizing that the theologians who thought it up had never been married and had never to

propound such advice in the confessional to married people
and avoid laughter.

In the early 1960s, after the development of the birth
control pill and with the announcement that a special papal
commission had been established to consider, outside the
context of the council, the birth control issue, the pill
became the de facto most popular form of birth limitation
among American Catholics (just as sterilization has become
now the most popular form of Catholic contraception). A decision had been made, with a sigh of relief, by a considerable number of American Catholics that the pill and the
papal commission had resolved the dilemma of having to
choose to between their church and their marriage (as they
perceived the dilemma). Moreover, their clergy, having read
the report of the majority of the birth control commission
in The National Catholic Reporter (most laity didn't know
there was a National Catholic Reporter, much less read it
but it was widely read at that time by the clergy, particularly by the clergy who were sympathetic to the prospect of
a change on contraception) aided and abetted the shifting
attitude among the lay people. The standard question when

confronted with the issue was, "Do you in your own
conscience think it is all right to practice birth control?"

The lay people would normally respond yes, in their
conscience they did think it was all right and the priests
would then say, "I am going to respect your conscience."
For the first time in their lives American Catholics found
that they were not only being asked but indeed forced to decide their own conscience and thus to work out a decision
between themselves and God. Given the power of sexual at-
traction in the human condition, small wonder that they began to imagine God more graciously than they had been taught
in grammar school, or high school, or in religious education
classes, or in Sunday sermons.

Then, to everyone's dismay (though not to the shock of
those who had followed closely), the birth control encyclical was issued in the summer of 1968. All the previous anguish was brought back and with a vengeance. During the
next six years some sixteen percentage points of American
Catholics who had been regular church attenders drifted away
from regular attendance (though only in a few cases to no
attendance at all). The others, encouraged and supported by
their parish priests, renewed their previous decision:
Because they believed in a loving and gracious God they did

not have to choose between, as they saw it, their marriage and their church.

Let me hasten to add, once again and perhaps tediously, that I am NOT saying that this was the way American Catholics and their clergy SHOULD have acted. I am saying it was the way, at least hypothetically, that they DID act and that having acted that way I can think of no response from the institutional leadership of the church which is likely to change either the lay people's attitude on birth control, or to modify the more gracious and benign image of God which they acquired as a result of the anguish of the multiple decisions they had to make in the middle and late sixties and early seventies about their church and their marriage and their God.

There were two, related, shifts between 1960 and 1969 that made possible and perhaps even inevitable the scenario which I have described. First of all, the council itself by introducing change into the church created an atmosphere, an environment, a climate of hope for more change. Secondly, the clergy were even more affected by this climate of hope for more change and more likely to change their minds themselves BEFORE THE LAITY DID. The council, in other words, heightened the lay people's expectations of change on birth

birth control and also changed the minds of an overwhelming proportion of the clergy before the issuing of Humanae Vitae. The environment created by the Council made possible, and perhaps inevitable, the response of the laity and the clergy to the birth control encyclical and the resulting sharp but brief decline in church practice, the long term decrease in acceptance of the sexual ethic and increase in gracious images of God. How would the laity have reacted to a birth control encyclical without the council? The question does not admit of answer because if it hadn't been for the council, the birth control commission would never have been set up and the encyclical would never have been necessary.

To put the matter yet another way, before the middle and late 1960s the majority of American Catholics were prepared to admit that birth control was a sin, even though many of them didn't think it was a sin like other sins, it was still something they had to confess and promise to try to avoid before they could receive Holy Communion. Because of the council, the establishment of the birth control commission, the expectation of change in the church and the changing values of the clergy, by the early 1970s almost nine-tenths of American Catholics did not think birth

control was a sin at all. Somehow or the other in the process they also changed their minds on premarital sex, not
only divorcing sex from procreation but divorcing it, in
some cases anyway, from permanent and public marital
commitment.

Are there any cautious recommendations a sociologist
(THIS sociologist) might make at the end of such a paradox-
ical analysis of American Catholicism since the end of the
Second Vatican Council?

I have four modest suggestions -- and it is an indication of the nature of the turmoil in the church today and of
the collapse of conversation between the upper church and
the lower church (the subject of one of my recommendations) that the American hierarchy cannot, without causing
enormous trouble for itself with Rome, discuss these recommendations, cannot even admit they have been made.

1. The leadership of the church ought to strive to establish institutions of upward communication by which it can
listen more closely and more sensitively to the laity's experience of God and life. Theologically this might be
called consulting the faithful, or discerning the spirit, or
ascertaining the "consensus fidelium." Pope John Paul in
his exhortation Familiaris consortio has said, as I noted

before, explicitly that the laity have a unique and indispensable contribution to make to the church's self-awareness in matters related to marriage. One would argue, however, only with blindness to the facts that the laity have been given an opportunity to make their unique and indispensable contribution. It is important to understand today that American Catholics are not saying that birth control and premarital sex is sinful but they're going to do it anyway -- they are, rather, saying that it is not sinful to divorce sex from procreation and even sex from permanent commitment. Apparently they have most of their clergy on their side in the first assertion and many of their clergy on their side in the second assertion. Thus far the hierarchy and the papacy have responded by saying in effect, "You're wrong, that's all. There's nothing to discuss because you're wrong!"

(Personally, I think I can understand what they're saying when they say that the experience of marriage persuades them that sex can be divorced from procreation. I also think that most of the data from the human sciences, comparative primatology, teleo-anthropology, etc., lends some support for this position. I will admit however, that I really don't understand their apparent insistence that sex

can be divorced from permanent and public commitment. I do
not believe that premarital sex is the greatest evil in the
world by any means but I am astonished that so many of the
laity so quickly have come to the conclusion that it isn't
really very evil at all.)

I am not suggesting that the institutional church simply cave in to this insistence of the laity that it misun-
derstands the human experience of sex, I am merely
recommending, as Archbishop John R. Quinn did in his address
at the synod on the family in 1980 that there be dialogue
between the laity and the hierarchy on this subject in which
the hierarchy listen carefully and try to discern perhaps
more sensitively than it has hitherto what the Holy Spirit
might be saying to the church through, to quote John Paul
again, "the unique and indispensable contribution" of the
married laity.

Will such dialogue happen? Of course not -- and hence
the non-dialogue and the turbulence and the crises will
continue.

2. It would be helpful if scholars and leaders, theologians and teachers, artists and writers, bent their efforts to development of a positive, constructive approach to
human sexuality in which the church was seen as clearly

supporting the attempts of the married lay people to grow in love of one another and of God through their marital intimacy. To sustain sexual passion (which is a sacrament of God's passionate love for us) through the long years of a marriage requires patience, sensitivity, discipline, tenderness, courage, vulnerability and the perennial willingness to start anew, to begin again, to be reborn. There is no reason to think that men and women living in the post-Freudian era have any more skills at these difficult virtues than did their predecessors. But surely the church has something to say about the motivations required to develop such skills. John Paul II's audience talks on human sexuality having set the context and provided the raw material and philosophical and theological reflection, now would certainly be the proper time for the church to encourage, support, facilitate and even push the development of such a positive and constructive theory of sexuality. No less a person than Cardinal Bernardin suggested that at the synod on the family -- and seems to have been ignored by everyone.

There is so much anger, resentment, bitterness, sullen and stubborn animosity, that no one, neither the hierarchy nor the theologians nor the clergy nor, with few exceptions,

writers, artists and story tellers, are going even to attempt such a positive theory of sexuality until they sniff
some winds of change from Rome, winds for which they surely
will sniff in vain for the imaginable future. This refusal
to do what is well within the capacity of the heritage to
begin to do seems to me to be comparable to the loss of
nerve among the clergy and the loss of confidence among
Catholic educators. Even though Catholic schools are more
important than they ever were and priests are more important
than they ever were, both the educators and the clergy refuse to abandon their crisis of identity. And, even though
the time is especially appropriate to develop a positive and
constructive Catholic theory of sexuality, those who might
be able to do so adamantly and stubbornly refuse to begin.
Their attitude often seems to be that they'll "be damned if
we'll do it, until the church changes on birth control." It
seems to me to be a foolish position but it is one that is
not going to be changed. Better to cheer for the
Sandanistas and for other Marxist/ Leninist regimes around
the world, than to work on a positive Catholic theory of
sex.

    3. Since the religious imagination is so important and
since the Catholic religious sensibility has changed so

notably in the last twenty years, it would make sense, would
it not, for the institutional church to begin to take more
seriously those works which have impact primarily on the
imagination -- art, music, literature, sculpture, architecture. Knowing that there is not the chance of an ice cube
in purgatory that anyone will take this recommendation seriously, I would nonetheless recommend in the time of an
emerging new religious sensibility that the church renew its
traditional commitment to the arts, fine and lively, that
was once so much taken for granted that no one would have
dreamed it possible the church would have abandoned the arts
as it has. The artist (musician, story teller, poet) is a
"sacrament maker," a person who calls out of his materials
insights and images into the meaning that lurks beneath
them. For most of its history the Catholic Church has realized that the sacrament makers are not luxuries but necessi-
ties for its life and work. One would like to think that as
a new religious sensibility develops the church leadership
will understand that the only way it can guide and direct
the development of that religious sensibility is not de-
nouncing it, not trying to limit it or contain it, but rather influencing its direction and flow through works of the
fine and lively arts.

4. Since the quality of Sunday preaching is such an important influence in the life of the lay people and since they rate that quality so low, It might be wise to attempt to improve the quality of preaching. The synod after the Extraordinary Synod is to be devoted to the laity. The laity themselves will not of course participate, save perhaps through carefully chosen and untypical tokenism; if the American Catholic laity were permitted to participate and the subject of Sunday preaching was raised, they would probably talk of no other subject until the bishops went home.

I know from previous experience that I might as well cut paper dolls out of the pages of this book as to recommend that something be done about the poor homilies the laity must sit through every weekend. The bishops and the clergy are now greatly exercised about the rights of the poor, but singularly disinterested in the right of the laity to have the gospel effectively preached to them, a right in strict commutative justice with an obligation to restitution.

Other people are bound to justice, it would seem, not Sunday homilists.

Better sermons, more concern about works of the imagination, a positive theory of sexual intimacy, more careful
attention to the actual experience of the laity -- surely
not an unreasonable agenda of policy issues.

Not unreasonable, but in the present condition of the
American Catholic bishops who will be represented at the
Synod, merely impossible.

The media image already created for the Extraordinary
Synod is that it is designed to rubber stamp efforts by Pope
John Paul II to revoke the Second Vatican Council. Despite
carefully worded denials, this image persists. Those attending the Synod should be aware -- though in all probability
they will not be -- that the news stories with this paradigm
in them are as good as written. Unless there is a dramatic
effort to shake that image, the Catholic people of the
United States will be told by the media and will believe
that the Synod went along with the Pope's determination to
"set the clock back."

I doubt that any so simplistic paradigm accurately de-
scribes either the Pope's motives or what will be the results of the synod. However, as Bishops don't seem to
comprehend, if the media report a misinterpretation, that

report becomes far more real than the reality mis-
interpreted.

In fact, the more probable result of the Synod, based
on earlier Synods, is that the Bishops will tell the Pope
not what he needs to know but what they think he wants to
hear. If the American delegation offers a picture appreciably different from that presented in this volume, they'd
better have high quality data to back up the picture or I'll
confront them with the charge of not telling the truth.

Should there actually be a desire to undue the Vatican
Council -- in letter or spirit -- this report would suggest
that it will have little impact. The leadership of the
Church can persecute the clergy, the religious, the Catholic
universities if it so chooses. Even in the last, however, it
can hardly affect the lay faculty.

The more vulnerable a religious or a cleric is the easier a target such a person may be for an ecclesiastical reaction to the Vatican Council. Thus cloistered religious
women can probably be pushed around more readily than anyone
else.

However, a reign of terror, a curial Thermidor, will
only offend the laity (mildly since it will not affect their

lives directly) and not cause them to return to the old ecclesiastical discipline. In the long run such a reaction
will only make a chaotic church more chaotic.

The data in this report should suggest to the Bishops
-- but probably won't -- that a new era is too far begun to
be undone and that in this era, likely to be around in the
United States for a long time, leaders will be required to
lead by sensitive listening and intelligent, nuanced response, not by giving orders and expecting automatic
obedience.

GRAPHS

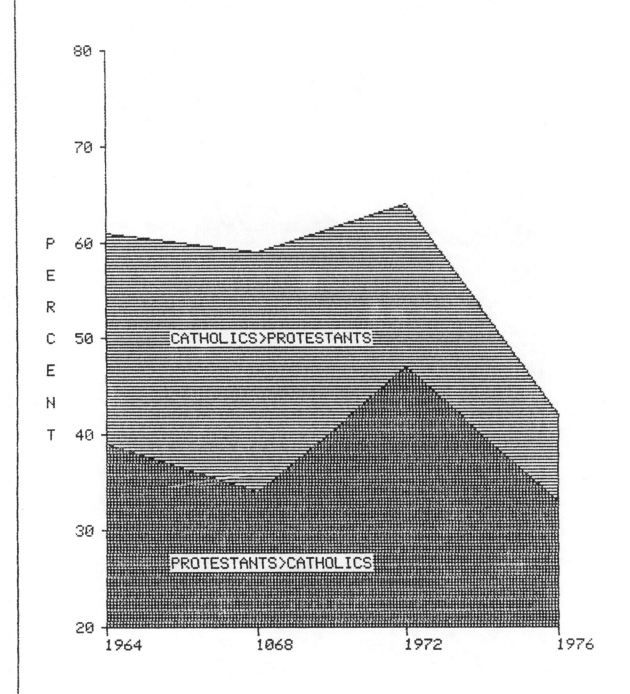

WARM FEELINGS(OVER 70)BETWEEN CATHS AND PROTS

CATHOLICS>PROTESTANTS

PROTESTANTS>CATHOLICS

P
E
R
C
E
N
T

80

70

60

50

40

30

20

1964   1068   1972   1976

YEAR

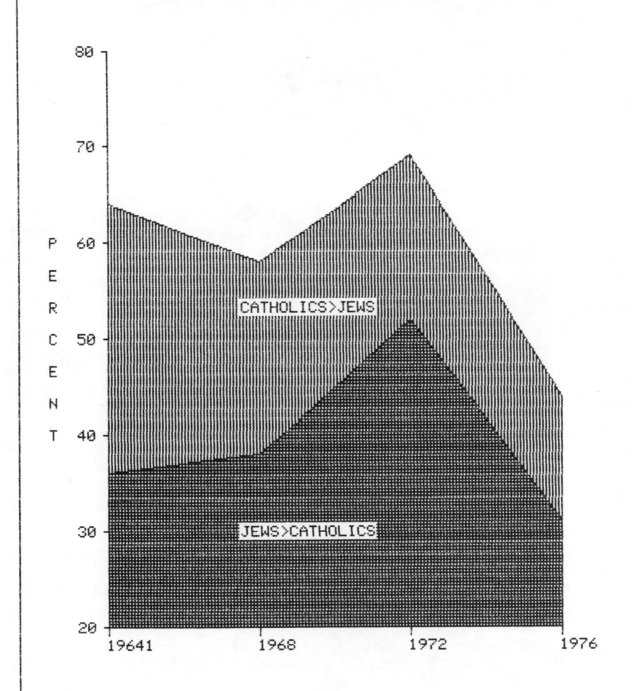

WARM FEELINGS (OVER 70)BETWEEN CATHOLICS AND JEWS

CATHOLICS>JEWS

JEWS>CATHOLICS

80

70

60

50

40

30

20

P
E
R
C
E
N
T

19641   1968   1972   1976

YEAR

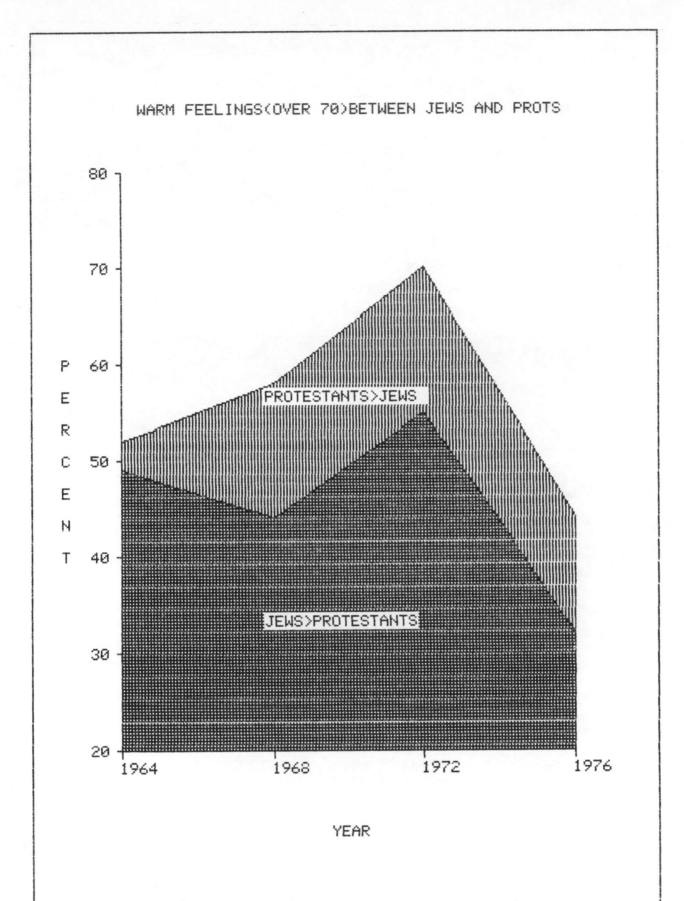

HOUSE VOTE BY RELIGION IN PRESIDENTIAL YEARS

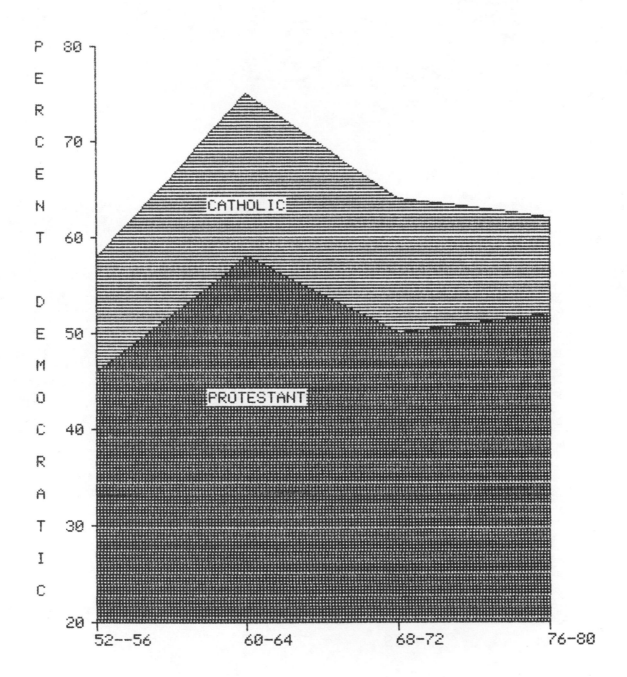

YEAR

PRESIDENTIAL VOTE BY RELIGION

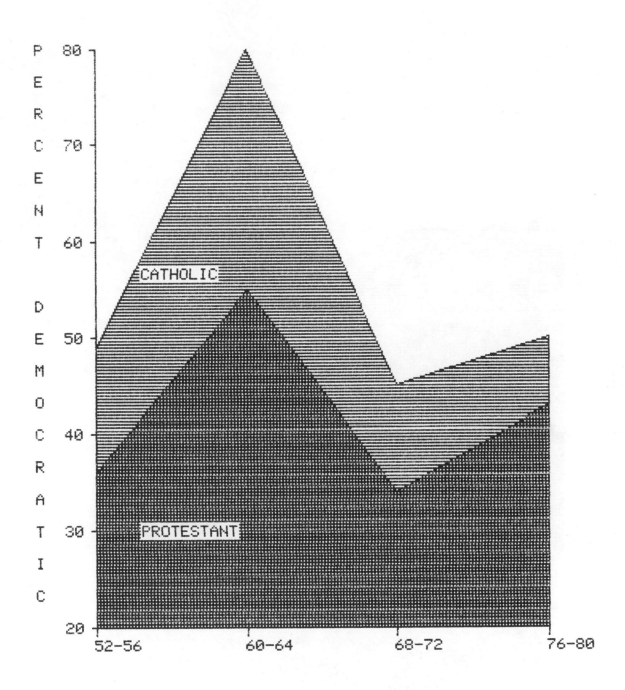

PARYID BY RELIGION AND YEAR

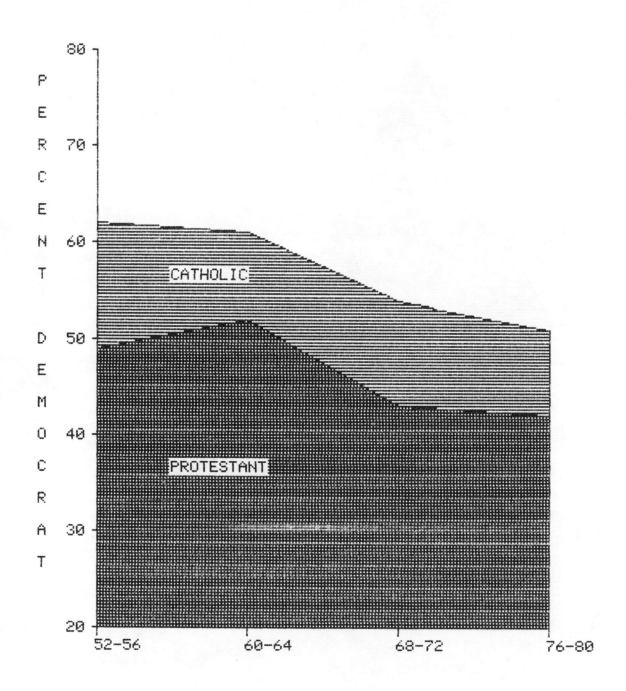

YEAR

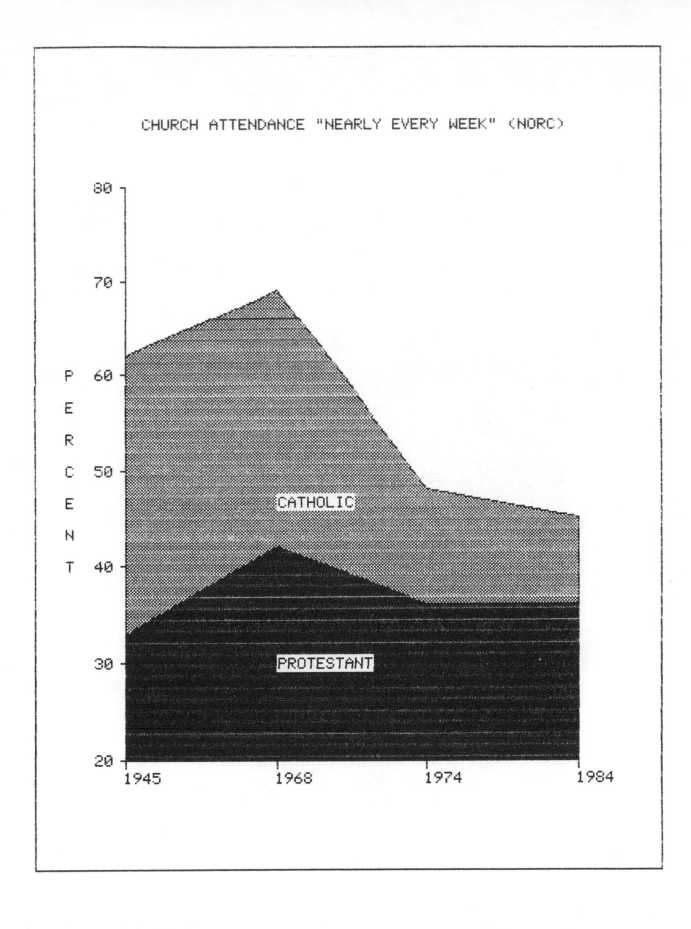

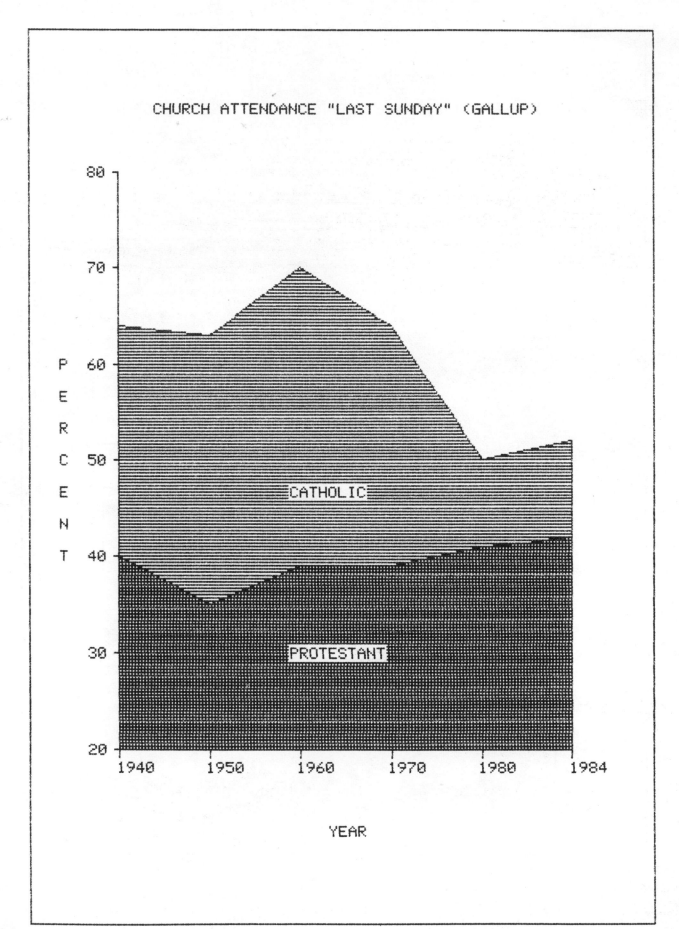